The *myspeedystudy* series of textbooks follow a down-to-earth way of teaching to disentangle the technical jargon typical for advanced finance and accounting topics. *myspeedystudy* makes complex subjects understandable and implements an easy to follow approach.

While the language and layout used in the *myspeedystudy* series of textbooks is precise and well-structured, it does so without sliding towards an artificially entertaining and flippant language. It is a timesaver for business students and professionals in Bachelor, Master and MBA and Executive classes.

Winfried Heinrichson

myspeedystudy

Introduction to IFRS Accounting

A very basic introduction

Bibliographic information published by the Deutsche Nationalbibliothek

The Deutsche Nationalbibliothek lists this publication in the Deutsche Nationalbibliografie; detailed bibliographic data are available on the Internet at http://dnb.dnb.de

Cover design: Winfried Heinrichson
© 2017 Winfried Heinrichson
Copyright with the author:
Winfried Heinrichson
c/o Cologne Business School
Hardefuststr. 1
50677 Köln
Printed by: Amazon Distribution GmbH, Leipzig
ISBN: 978-1-5237-4007-9

About the book

This book is a very basic introduction to IFRS. It is not written with the intention to educate upcoming auditing or accounting professionals – though they might find some interesting thoughts and explanations in here not to be found in more rigorous textbooks. The book has been written for students (graduates, bachelor, master, MBA) in business programs where subjects like International Accounting are part of a general curriculum and taught in only one semester. These students should get a good overview of the concepts and important standards of the IFRS – and eventually find their way to more specialized classes and literature.

An introductory textbook cannot provide an exhaustive or in-depth overview of IFRS – but after studying the book, students should be well-equipped with enough knowledge for later practical use or further studies.

The *myspeedystudy* series of textbooks follow a down-to-earth way of teaching to disentangle the technical and mathematical jargon typical for advanced finance topics. *myspeedystudy* aims to make complex subjects understandable and implements an easy to follow step-by-step approach. While the language and layout used in the *myspeedystudy* series of textbooks is precise and well-structured, it does so without sliding towards an artificially entertaining and flippant language. It is a timesaver for business students and professionals in Bachelor, Master and MBA and Executive classes.

Cologne, February 2017   Winfried Heinrichson

Contents

List of examples

1   A quick introduction

1.1   What is this book about

The purpose of this text is to explain the principles of "International Accounting Standards" (IAS) or International Financial Reporting Standards (IFRS).

The international standard-setting process began several decades ago as an effort by industrialized nations to create standards that could also be used by developing and smaller nations unable to establish their own accounting standards. But as the business world became more global, regulators, investors, large companies and auditing firms began to realize the importance of having common standards in all areas of the financial reporting chain.

Today, the globalization of business and finance has led to more than 100 countries to adopt and then to require or allow the use of IFRS for the preparation of financial statements by publicly held companies. It is reasonable to believe that common global reporting standards are necessary to produce credible, comparable, conceptually sound, and useful financial information – information used by managers, investors, and creditors of make certain decisions.

IFRS are a set of international accounting standards issued by the International Accounting Standards Board in London (IASB) stating how particular types of transactions and other events should be reported in financial statements.

IFRS are sometimes confused with IAS (International Accounting Standards), which are the older standards that IFRS replaced. IAS (International Accounting Standards) were issued from 1973 to 2000, but after 2000 the IASB figured that IAS (the "A" stands for Accounting) does not fully reflect the purpose of the standards – so they replaced the "A" (Accounting) in IAS with "FR" (Financial Reporting), so that the new standards would be called IFRS.

Many countries have delegated the task of setting accounting standards to the International Accounting Standards Board (IASB):

- Since 2005 EU companies that have their shares traded on a public exchange must prepare their consolidated financial statements in accordance with International Financial Reporting Standards (IFRS) as promulgated by the IASB and endorsed by the European Union. Most EU countries, however, also have their own national accounting standard-setting bodies. These bodies may, for example, set accounting standards for private companies and for single entity financial statements of public companies or comment on the IASB's drafts of new or modified standards.

- Since 2005 and 2007, respectively, Australian and New Zealand public companies must comply with locally adopted IFRS, labeled A-IFRS and NZ-IFRS. These sets of standards include all IFRS requirements as well as some additional disclosure requirements.

- South African public companies have prepared financial statements that comply with IFRS, as published by the IASB, since 2005.

- Some other countries with major stock exchanges requiring (most) publicly listed companies to prepare IFRS compliant financial statements are Brazil (since 2010) Canada (2011), and Korea (2011).

- Thailand has long been aware that convergence with international accounting and financial reporting standards is a necessary step to remain competitive as an investment destination in both the regional and global economy. The Federation of Accounting Profession ('FAP') Committee of Thailand has considered and approved a roadmap to develop Thai Financial Reporting Standards ('TFRS') in line with International Financial Reporting Standards ('IFRS').

Who should read this book

- Anyone in business who has to deal with published accounts and internal reports now or in the future; or who is responsible for reports that are affected by or lead to published accounts. This includes professional advisers, directors and executive officers from functions other than finance are affected by the requirements of Accounting Standards.

- Students who are studying accounting as a non-specialist subject, for example on a business studies or engineering course. The text will serve as a basic reference book to be used throughout the course. It will also be particularly helpful in providing the basic grounding which is required before moving on to the more technical and in-depth study of the subject that may be required in some courses.

- Accountants and students of accountancy will find this text useful as an overview of Accounting Standards, as it cuts through to what the Standards aim to achieve and thus what has to be accounted for and disclosed; and

- Non-financial managers, who need an appreciation of the purposes and use of accounting information. It covers the basic principles of financial accounting for those who do not require detailed technical knowledge. The text will enable the reader to contribute in the workplace or to progress to further financial studies.

What you should know already – in an ideal world

Readers *should definitely be familiar* with the basics of double-entry bookkeeping and the nature of financial statements. Double-entry bookkeeping will not be explained in this book. Double-entry bookkeeping is based on the idea that any business transaction (an income, an expense, a change in the assets or liabilities of the company) should be recorded in (at least) two accounts. Accounts are used to record the financial effect of the transactions that take place during the year and to create the prerequisite to determine a profit of the year.

1.2   What you have to learn

This section will give an overview on what you would have to learn, and why.

1.2.1   Terminology

All subjects have and use their specific language – so does Financial Accounting. Only in Financial Accounting we have to be a little careful, because Financial Accounting uses terms which can also be used in everyday conversation for all kinds of economic situations – like cost, liquidity, assets, profit, valuation, debt and many more.

In Financial Accounting these terms usually have very specific meanings, and we should be careful not to mix them up with what we think they might mean in an everyday situation. Apart from that, specialists enjoy speaking their own jargon – not only because they feel so special, but mostly because it will save time, if knowledgeable people discuss things.

1.2.2   The scope of financial reporting

Accounting standards and rules limit management's ability to misuse accounting judgment by regulating how particular types of transactions are recorded.

These **accounting standards,** which are designed to convey quantitative information on a firm's performance, are complemented by a set of **disclosure principles.** The disclosure principles guide the amount and kinds of information that is disclosed and require a firm to provide qualitative information related to assumptions, policies, and uncertainties that underlie the quantitative data presented.

1.2.3   Concepts and some theory

Students are sometimes irritated about the various objectives, purposes, rules and elements of financial statements.

Experience shows that it will be easier for students to understand any accounting rule in general and the rules of IFRS in particular the more they understand the structure, the underlying concepts and the purposes of accounting. So let's start with the general structure of the standards.

Accounting Concepts and Principles are a set of broad conventions that have been developed over time to provide a framework for financial reporting. As financial reporting involves significant professional judgments by accountants, these concepts and principles ensure that the users of financial information are not mislead by the adoption of accounting policies and practices that go against the spirit of the accountancy profession. Accountants must therefore actively consider whether the accounting treatments adopted are consistent with the accounting concepts and principles. Students should start and get acquainted with the terms in Table 1-1.

Table 1-1 Important terms used in accounting standards

Recognition	*Measurement*	*Disclosure*
Refers to the process of deciding whether an item has to be put into the financial statements (balance sheet, income statement, cash flow statement or other) or not. An item being "recognized" means it is being put into any of the financial statements.	Once it has been decided that an item is to be recognized, it has to be decided with which value. The process of associating monetary amounts to the items is called measurement.	Not all information will find its way into the main financial statements. It may well be that certain information is not recognized in the financial statements, but it may well be important enough to be shown in the accompanying notes. Disclosure refers to the process of deciding exactly which and where certain information is to be shown.

Measurement	
Initial measurement	*Subsequent measurement*
On initial recognition – so when an item is entered into the financial statements for the first time – assets or liabilities are measured according to the value concept applicable to that item laid out in the appropriate standard. This value concept may be for example *cost* or *fair value*.	When those assets or liabilities are initially recognized, at every balance sheet date they need to be again measured. Now different value concepts may be applied. For example non-current assets will have to be depreciated. All assets will eventually have to be impaired. Provisions may be subject to accretion.

Concepts determining profit of the year	
Revenue Recognition	*Expense Recognition*
- Revenues are inflows of assets (or settlements of liabilities!) resulting from providing a product or service to a customer. - The timing of revenue recognition is a key element of earnings measurement, because it is not always obvious in which period a revenue is to be recognized. - Not adhering to revenue recognition criteria could result in overstating revenue and hence net income in one reporting period and, consequently, understating revenue and net income in another period.	- Expenses outflows or other using up of assets or incurrences of liabilities. Expense recognition often matches revenues and that arise from the same transactions or other events. - The net result is a measure – net income—that identifies the amount of profit or loss for the period provided by operations. - Some expenses are not incurred directly to produce a particular amount of revenue. Instead, the association between revenue and many expenses is indirect. Therefore, expense recognition is implemented by one of four different approaches, explained in later sections.

Relationship between Financial Accounting and Tax Accounting	
Financial Accounting	**Tax Accounting**
Enterprises are required (either by law or because they are listed on national stock exchanges) to follow financial accounting and reporting rules aimed at providing investors with a true and fair view of the financial situation of the enterprise. Financial accounting and reporting rules are increasingly based on a fair presentation approach.	The results shown for financial purposes (normally the consolidated group results) may differ considerably from the profits shown in the books of single enterprises or in the tax returns. This is because tax laws can be interpreted as rules to determine a taxable profit – and governments have the objective to preserve the tax base. Some countries, in particular in Continental Europe, follow the concept of dependence in determining the taxable results. Germany for example takes the profits resulting from the commercial accounts as the primary basis for tax assessment ("Maßgeblichkeitsprinzip"). Subject to the relevant taxation rules, certain fiscal adjustments have to be made in order to calculate the taxable profits.

- One consequence is that companies have to prepare at least two profit calculations – one for financial reporting and one for taxation purposes. For those new to the world of accounting, the idea that there are different "profits" for the same period sounds weird. But get used to this: there is no objective profit. Profit is a highly subjective concept and depends very much on the rules being applied to measure it – such as depreciation and amortization rules, inventory measurement rules or provision measurement rules.
- Another consequence may be that corporations are more confronted with unwarranted requests for tax profits adjustments or with the requirement that profits shown for financial purposes in a given country be taxable in that country.

1.3 The case for international reporting standards

Financial statements and reports for shareholders and other users are prepared using principles, rules or laws that can be interpreted in different ways. To ensure that these rules (or laws) are interpreted in the same or at least similar way, some form of regulation is required. Taxable profits are usually based on accounting profit and the number and type of adjustments required to compute taxable profits out of accounting profits varies from country to country.

- In some countries taxable income is closely linked to the accounting profit - e.g. in Germany it still is – and accounting rules are largely driven by taxation laws. These countries are usually known as code law countries, countries where the legal system originated in Roman law. These countries tend to have detailed laws relating to trading entities and accounting standards are usually embodied within the law. Accounting regulation in these countries is usually in the hands of the government and financial reporting is a matter of complying with a set of legal rules.
- In other countries the common law system is used. Common law is based on case law and tends to have less detailed regulations. In countries with common law systems, the

accounting regulation within the legal system is usually kept to a minimum, with detailed accounting regulations produced by professional organizations or other private sector accounting standard-setting bodies.

Whichever system is adopted, there is a need for every country to have a system for regulating the preparation of financial statements and reports.

Accounting and the financial reports derived from the accounting system provides companies, investors, regulators and others with a standardized way to describe the financial performance of an entity. Accounting standards are set of rules to which preparers of financial statements shall adhere to put together an entity's accounts. Companies listed on public stock exchanges are legally required to publish financial statements in accordance with the relevant accounting standards.

International Financial Reporting Standards (IFRS) is a single set of accounting standards, developed and maintained by the IASB in London with the intention of those standards being applied on a globally consistent basis — by developed, emerging and developing economies — thus providing investors and other users of financial statements with the ability to compare the financial performance of publicly listed companies on a like-for-like basis with their international peers.

Stock markets rely on published financial information by entities. Banks and family members are usually in a position to demand information directly from the entity or directly from management, whereas shareholders of publicly traded corporations have to rely on publicly available information.

Then, with the increase of international, cross-border investments by large publicly traded corporations it seems that the ultimate objective of the efforts at setting global standards for accounting and financial reporting is to make corporate financial reports comparable, regardless of their geographical origin. This has been increasingly important in the case of multinational companies when operating internationally and using different sets of reporting standards which made it less efficient to compare the financial statements. Another importance for harmonization has been an increasing focus on investors as they benefit from new IFRS due to investor oriented approach.

However, setting global standards alone is not sufficient to achieve this objective. Accounting scandals happen anywhere in the world, and the reasons for this to happen are more complicated than just the nature of the accounting standards used. Effective enforcement is equally important as the type of regulation or accounting standard used, and that enforcement effectiveness is influenced by such factors as the availability of adequate resources for the enforcement agencies, and their level of independence from political interference.

In this context, these three terms should be learned and understood by students:

Harmonization

Harmonization refers to a process of *reducing unnecessary differences in accounting across countries*, while retaining a degree of flexibility. Harmonization allows different countries to have different standards as long as the standards do not conflict. Initial efforts focused on harmonization—reducing differences among the accounting principles used in major capital markets around the world. The goal is to achieve some level of comparability in the way financial statements are prepared and presented. When international harmonization occurs, the difficulties for companies and individuals considerably decrease in presenting the financial statements and their interpretations. There are several organizations that have been trying to eliminate the differences between financial reporting standards and achieve international harmonization. If international harmonization is achieved, many countries would benefit from it as it would improve the access to the international financial markets and improve the confidence and knowledge of investors which may even trigger an increase in future investments.

Convergence

By the 1990s, the notion of harmonization was replaced by the concept of **convergence**—*the development of a unified set of high-quality*, international accounting standards that would be used in at least all major capital markets. International convergence of accounting standards is not a new idea. The concept of convergence first arose in the late 1950s in response to post World War II economic integration and related increases in cross-border capital flows.

Standardization

Standardization, on the other hand, implies *a complete elimination of alternatives with all countries following the same standards*. So standardization is the process of unifying the reporting standards to make them the same.

How can countries adopt IFRS?

The following is an overview over the different ways and scenarios in which international accounting rules can be implemented by countries.

Table 1-2: Scenarios for the adoption of international accounting rules

Type of adoption	relevant for
replace national GAAP with IFRS	every entity using national GAAP
use IFRS in preparing consolidated financial statements	only parent companies, since consolidated statements have only to be prepared by companies owning other companies
use IFRS in preparing consolidated financial statements	as an additional factor, requirement to use IFRS could be determined for companies using a regulated capital market (stock or bond market)
use IFRS	foreign companies listed on domestic stock exchange
use IFRS	domestic companies listing on foreign stock exchanges

1.4   Accounting information and the three basic questions

The list of people who might need the information provided by financial statements seems long – for good reasons. Some of these people are directly connected with the organization, for example its employees and managers, others are not directly connected but they may be affected by its management of finance or its financial stability, for example the general public. The people who are – or in some cases should – be interested in the information provided by financial statements include:

- Existing owners or shareholders of the company and prospective investors
- Managers, current and prospective employees
- Union representatives
- Lenders, potential lenders, suppliers and customers
- The government
- The public
- Journalists, analysts and advisers.

Most companies publish at least three financial statements once a year. Publicly listed companies do this quarterly, others annually. These financial statements consist of the income statement, the balance sheet and the cash flow statement (and more). In general terms these help to provide the answers to three basic questions about a company. No matter which user group we are considering, it is possible to express in very general terms the questions that most users will be asking when they are reviewing a company's published financial statements. Whoever reads these financial statements for professional reasons will be trying to find answers to one or more of the following three questions.

Question 1: What is the profit situation of the firm?

The owners and potential investors want to know how much profit they can earn from their investment in the business. Also, the government is interested in the profit – since they will collect part of that as income taxes. Make yourself familiar with the idea that accounting rules on the one hand and tax laws on the other hand are just two different sets of rules to determine profit – with the consequence that the profit will be calculated differently for the owners and the tax authorities.

Competitors will be interested in whether the firm is earning a higher or lower return than they are achieving themselves. All these people want to know:

- What sales revenue is the firm generating? The sales revenue is an indicator of the company's success to bring products or services to its relevant market.
- What expenses are they incurring in generating that revenue, and do the expenses exceed the revenue?

- If the organization is making a profit, what have they decided to do with it? How much has been reinvested in the business for future growth? How much has been taken out of the business by the owners as dividends?

Question 2: What is the risk associated with the firm?

An existing or a potential lender will be interested in the risk that the firm represents as a borrower – the risk of default, i.e. that the firm is not able to pay interest or repay the loan.

And not only banks or bond holders are creditors. Suppliers can be creditors too, as they send goods or deliver services with payment due later. Even customers can be interpreted as creditors – since economically and legally they may expect future services or warranties provided by the firm. It happens that potential customers request financial statements from their prospective supplier – so that they can assess the supplier's financial strength and probability of survival.

All these parties will ask themselves questions like:

- What does the organization owe to other entities (already) and what is the financial burden associated with the existing debt?
- What is the financial flexibility of the firm?
- What valuable assets does the firm possess as security for a loan?
- How much of the business's capital is borrowed and how much has been invested by the owners?

Question 3: What about the liquidity of the firm?

Every firm needs cash to pay bills, to invest, to pay dividends or to repay debt.

Get used to the idea that there are situations for a firm in which they generate profits and they still are short on cash. These situations happen. On the other hand, companies not making any profits can have plenty of cash. This also happens, often with newly founded companies being financed by huge capital injections from shareholders. And of course, there are companies making huge profits and piling up tons of cash at the same time. Everything is possible. So – making profits does not mean having sufficient cash and vice versa.

Readers of financial statements might ask:

- How much cash – if at all - does the firm generate from its operating activities? Or does the organization burn cash – which is often the case for newly founded companies.
- Is there sufficient cash to cover the firm's investment for future growth? How does the firm obtain the cash for investments?
- If there is not sufficient cash from the firm's own activities, what sources are used to make up for the cash needed, but is not generated by the activities of the firm?

2   Fundamental accounting concepts

2.1   The IASC/IASB conceptual framework

A *conceptual framework* establishes the concepts that underlie financial reporting. A conceptual framework is a coherent system of concepts derived from **objectives**. From objectives we can identify the **purpose** of financial reporting.

Accounting concepts and rules provide guidance on

(1) identifying the boundaries of financial reporting;

(2) selecting the transactions, other events, and circumstances to be represented;

(3) how they should be recognized and measured; and

(4) how they should be summarized and reported.

A conceptual framework enables the IASB as a standard-setting body to issue consistent pronouncements over time, from which a coherent set of standards should result. Otherwise standard-setting might end up being based on individual concepts developed by each member of the standard-setting body.

The IASB's conceptual framework is described in the document, "Framework for Preparation and Presentation of Financial Statements." Its first level identifies the objective of financial reporting—that is, the purpose of financial reporting. The second level provides the qualitative characteristics that make accounting information useful and the elements of financial statements (assets, liabilities, and so on). The third level identifies the recognition, measurement, and disclosure concepts used in establishing and applying accounting standards and the specific concepts to implement the objective. These concepts include assumptions, principles, and constraints that describe the present reporting environment.

Table 2-1 Framework for Financial Reporting

First level	Objective of Financial Reporting – Purpose of Accounting		
Second level	Qualitative Characteristics of accounting information	Elements of Financial Statements	
Third level	Recognition	Measurement	Disclosure

2.1.1 Objective of general purpose financial reporting

On the first level of the framework, the IASB describes the *objective of general purpose financial reporting as follows*:

The primary users of general purpose financial reporting are present and potential investors, lenders and other creditors, who use that information to make decisions about buying, selling or holding equity or debt instruments and providing or settling loans or other forms of credit. The primary users need information about the resources of the entity not only to assess an entity's prospects for future net cash inflows but also how effectively and efficiently management has discharged their responsibilities to use the entity's existing resources.

It also gives an overview of which items of information is perceived to be "decision useful":

Economic resources and claims (presented in the balance sheet)

Information about the nature and amounts of a reporting entity's economic resources and claims assists users to assess that entity's financial strengths and weaknesses; to assess liquidity and solvency, and its need and ability to obtain financing. Information about the claims and payment requirements assists users to predict how future cash flows will be distributed among those with a claim on the reporting entity.

Changes in economic resources and claims (presented in statement of comprehensive income)

Changes in a reporting entity's economic resources and claims result from that entity's performance and from other events or transactions such as issuing debt or equity instruments. Users need to be able to distinguish between both of these changes.

Financial performance reflected by accrual accounting

Information about a reporting entity's financial performance during a period, representing changes in economic resources and claims other than those obtained directly from investors and creditors, is useful in assessing the entity's past and future ability to generate net cash inflows. Such information may also indicate the extent to which general economic events have changed the entity's ability to generate future cash inflows.

Financial performance reflected by past cash flows (presented in the statement of cash flows)

Information about a reporting entity's cash flows during the reporting period also assists users to assess the entity's ability to generate future net cash inflows. This information indicates how the entity obtains and spends cash, including information about its borrowing and repayment of debt, cash dividends to shareholders.

Changes in economic resources and claims not resulting from financial performance (presented in the statement of changes in equity)

Information about changes in an entity's economic resources and claims resulting from events and transactions other than financial performance, such as the issue of equity instruments or distributions of cash or other assets to shareholders is necessary to complete the picture of the total change in the entity's economic resources and claims.

2.1.2   Qualitative Characteristics of useful financial information

The IASB has laid out what is considers to be the characteristics of *useful financial information*. These qualitative characteristics of useful financial reporting identify the types of information are likely to be most useful to users in making decisions about the reporting entity on the basis of information in its financial report. The qualitative characteristics apply equally to financial information in general purpose financial reports as well as to financial information provided in other ways. In chapter 3 of the framework the IASB describes how it understands information to be useful:

"Financial information is useful when it is relevant and represents faithfully what it purports to represent. The usefulness of financial information is enhanced if it is comparable, verifiable, timely and understandable."

Fundamental qualitative characteristics

Understandability: Information should be presented in a way that is readily understandable by users who have a reasonable knowledge of business and economic activities and accounting and who are willing to study the information diligently.

Timeliness is another component of *relevance*. To be useful, information must be provided to users within the time period in which it is most likely to bear on their decisions.

Reliability: Information in financial statements is reliable if it is free from material error and bias and can be depended upon by users to represent events and transactions faithfully. Information is not reliable when it is purposely designed to influence users' decisions in a particular direction.

Relevance: Information in financial statements is relevant when it influences the economic decisions of users. It can do that both by (a) helping them evaluate past, present, or future events relating to an enterprise and by (b) confirming or correcting past evaluations they have made. Financial information is capable of making a difference in decisions if it has predictive value, confirmatory value, or both. The predictive value and confirmatory value of financial information are interrelated.

Materiality is a component of *relevance*. Information is material if its omission or misstatement could influence the economic decisions of users. Materiality is based on the nature or magnitude (or both) of the items to which the information relates in the context of an individual entity's financial report.

Faithful representation. General purpose financial reports represent economic phenomena in words and numbers. To be useful, financial information must not only be relevant, it must also represent faithfully the phenomena it purports to represent. This fundamental characteristic seeks to maximize the underlying characteristics of completeness, neutrality and freedom from error. Information must be both relevant and faithfully represented if it is to be useful.

Enhancing qualitative characteristics

Comparability, verifiability, timeliness and understandability are qualitative characteristics that enhance the usefulness of information that is relevant and faithfully represented.

Comparability Information about a reporting entity is more useful if it can be compared with similar information about other entities and with similar information about the same entity for another period or another date. Comparability enables users to identify and understand similarities in, and differences among, items.

Verifiability helps to assure users that information represents faithfully the economic phenomena it purports to represent. Verifiability means that different knowledgeable and independent observers could reach consensus, although not necessarily complete agreement, that a particular depiction is a faithful representation.

Timeliness means that information is available to decision-makers in time to be capable of influencing their decisions.

Understandability Classifying, characterizing and presenting information clearly and concisely makes it understandable. While some phenomena are inherently complex and cannot be made easy to understand, to exclude such information would make financial reports incomplete and potentially misleading. Financial reports are prepared for users who have a reasonable knowledge of business and economic activities and who review and analyze the information with diligence.

The cost constraint on useful financial reporting

Cost is a pervasive *constraint* on the information that can be provided by general purpose financial reporting. Reporting such information imposes costs and those costs should be justified by the benefits of reporting that information.

Table 2-2 Hierarchy of Accounting Information

Basic assumptions	Accrual Basis and matching principle		Going concern	
Primary users of accounting information	Capital providers, Investors, Creditors			
Pervasive criterion	Decision Usefulness			

Fundamental qualitative characteristics	Relevance	Materiality	Reliability	Faithful representation

Enhancing qualitative characteristics	Verifiability	Comparability	Timeliness	Understandability
Cost constraint	Reporting information imposes costs and those costs should be justified by the benefits of reporting that information.			

Enhancing qualities	Completeness	Prudence Substance over form	Neutrality

2.2   Principle-based vs. Rule-based standards

Some debate exists regarding the issue of principles-based versus rules-based standards.

- Rules-based standards attempt to anticipate all or most of the application issues and prescribe solutions. As a result, U.S. GAAP as codified by the FASB consists of about 17,000 pages trying to solve most individual accounting and reporting scenarios that a company might encounter.

- Principles-based standards are less prescriptive and rely on broad statements of objectives and principles to be followed. Consequently, IFRS are contained in about 2,500 pages or about 15 percent as much as U.S. GAAP. Greater reliance is placed on the preparer's judgment to align the financial reporting with the conceptual framework.

- German Accounting, as laid out in the German Commercial Code (Handelsgesetzbuch), can be considered as a highly principles-based approach to accounting and reporting. The German Commercial Code even refers to partly uncoded "Grundsätze ordnungsmäßiger Buchführung" (loosely translated as "Principles of orderly bookkeeping") to be observed by firms.

It may be argued that with rule-based standards companies may have an incentive to structure agreements and transactions to achieve particular objectives which may not reflect the underlying substance ("Show me a rule that says that I can't do this"). For example, companies structure long-term lease agreements as operating leases when in substance they are finance leases. The result might be more "off-balance-sheet" financing.

Table 2-3: Perceived differences between rules- and principles-based standards

Attribute	Rules-based standards	Principles-based standards
Conceptual framework	Less important	More important
Professional judgment	Less important	More important
Level of detailed guidance	More	Less
Industry specific guidance	More	Less

2.3 Concept of capital maintenance

Capital maintenance is the idea to see whether an entity has managed to maintain its original financial capital over the accounting period, so if it is the same at the end of the year as it was at the start of the year. Any change to the capital can occur only if the company made a profit or a loss, or if there were injections or withdrawals made by the owners of the entity. So by comparing the capital at the end of the period with the capital at the beginning of the period, and correcting for capital infusions or withdrawals (e.g. dividend payments), we can find the profit or loss of the year.

The concept of capital maintenance is concerned with how an entity defines the capital that it seeks to maintain. What is exactly measured as being the financial capital of the entity?

What we need is *a point of reference by which profit is measured*; hence, profit is the residual amount that remains after expenses (including capital maintenance adjustments, where appropriate) have been deducted from income. If expenses exceed income, the residual amount is a loss.

After all, this is not a trivial question. If we interpret Net Income or Net Profit as the amount of wealth that can be taken away from the company by the owners as dividends without making the entity less wealthy as it was before – we see right away that measuring that income decides whether the company has decreased in wealth or not.

Usually we define as capital of a business the excess of its assets over its liabilities – which is equity. It represents the shareholder's interest in the business. One way of calculating profit is to compare the equity at the end of a period with the equity at the beginning of the period – and correcting it for withdrawals and injections of capital from owners.

- The withdrawals – e.g. dividends – would have to be added. They have decreased the equity, but they have not decreased profit – so they have to be added.

- The capital injections would have to be subtracted. New capital provided by owners has increased equity, but not profit – so capital injections have to be subtracted to calculate profit.

Let's look at a simplified scheme of profit calculation:

Equity at the end of the period
– equity at the beginning of the period
= total change of equity during the period
+ withdrawals by owners
– capital injections by owners
= profit of the period

Now, if equity is the result of the measurement of assets and liabilities, then the amount of profit is logically the consequence of how the business measures the value of the assets and the liabilities.

The *financial capital maintenance concept* assumes that a company has income only if the dollar amount of an enterprise's net assets (assets — liabilities or, in other words, owners' equity) at the end of a period exceeds the dollar amount of net assets at the beginning of the period after excluding the effects of transactions with owners.

Example 2-1: Financial Maintenance

Capital of Muck GmbH (net assets = assets minus liabilities) according to the financial statements at the end of the period war 70,000€, and 30,000€ at the beginning of the period. During the year, the owners of Muck GmbH have withdrawn 10,000€ as dividends, and they also invested 20,000€ from their own private money in the business. Income for the period would be 30,000€, computed as follows:

Net assets, end of period:	70,000€
– Net assets, beginning of period	– 30,000€
= Change (increase) in net assets	40,000€
+ add distributions to owners	+ 10,000€
– deduct investment by owners	– 20,000€
= Income	30,000€

The **physical capital maintenance concept** assumes that income occurs only if the *physical productive capacity of the enterprise* at the end of a period exceeds the physical productive capacity at the beginning of the same period, also after excluding the effects of transactions with owners.

This concept requires that productive assets (inventories, buildings, and equipment) be valued at *fair market values or current cost.* Productive capital is maintained only if the current costs of these capital assets are maintained. Consider the beginning net asset value of 30,000€ in the previous example. Now assume that, because of rising prices of buildings, inventory, equipment, and so forth, in order to maintain the same productive capacity (=being equally wealthy in terms of productive capacity) the company would have to have 34,000€ in net asset value by the end of the year. If the ending net asset value were 70,000€, as before, and new investments and dividends were as shown, income would be 26,000€ rather than 30,000€. The 4,000€ difference would be the amount necessary just to keep up with inflation, in order to "maintain physical productive capacity" and therefore would not be part of income.

2.4   Economic Entity

The business enterprise is viewed as a specific economic entity separate and distinct from its owners and any other business unit. The financial statements will therefore only include the assets and liabilities which are attributable to the business enterprise – and not to the owners.

Identifying the exact extent of the economic entity can be quite difficult with large corporations that have networks of subsidiaries and subsidiaries of subsidiaries with complex business ties among the members of the group.

But also at the other end of the spectrum, with very small businesses, it is often difficult to disentangle the owner's personal transactions from the transactions of that small business.

2.5   Arm's length transactions

Transactions are assumed to be arm's-length transactions. That is, they occur between independent parties, each of which is capable of protecting its own interests. The idea is that e.g. values (assets, liabilities, income, expenses) must not be distorted because one entity (the parent) can muscle the other entity (the subsidiary) to value transactions in a deceitful manner. Being able to exercise control in this way would not be what we consider to be "at arm's length".

2.6   *Going concern*

Accountants prepare financial statements under the assumption that the business is a *going concern.*

It means that the enterprise is expected to continue to trade in its present form for the foreseeable future. This contrasts with the assumption that a business is a 'gone concern', i.e., it is about to collapse, be liquidated or undergo other drastic transformation.

The significance of this distinction is that under the going-concern assumption the balance sheet values of a company's assets could be considered to be reasonably realistic, whereas under a liquidation assumption the value of the assets would be what they would eventually be worth in a sudden liquidation.

For example, if a company is expected to continue trading for the foreseeable future, its fixed assets, such as its plant and equipment, would have some value from being used helping to generate revenues and the corresponding balance sheet values could be regarded as a reasonable approximation of their value to the company based on the cost minus the accumulated depreciation.

In general, depreciation and amortization policies are justifiable and appropriate only if we assume some permanence to the company. If a company adopts the liquidation approach, the current/non-current classification of assets and liabilities loses much of its significance. Labeling anything a long-lived or non-current asset would be difficult to justify. Indeed, listing liabilities on the basis of priority in liquidation would be more reasonable.

On the other hand, if the company is expected to cease trading then its fixed assets could be expected to realize only a fraction of their balance sheet values if they were to be sold.

Likewise, its current assets are also likely to realize only a fraction of their balance sheet values – or as we call it in a more professional way – *carrying values.*

2.7   Measurement in monetary terms

An accounting item such as income, expenditure, asset or a liability will only be included in the accounts and in the financial statements if it can be assessed or measured in monetary terms. The monetary unit is considered relevant, simple, universally available, understandable, and useful.

This means that many of a company's intellectual assets, e.g., its staff and other personnel, its market share, its customer base – all very important and valuable to the company – are not included in its balance sheet. The reason for this is not difficult to understand. Companies find it almost impossible to place a monetary value on people, market shares or customer bases.

Sports clubs have an easier task because they at least can value the players that they buy at the price that they pay for such players. But as a matter of fact, sports club do not put the players in the balance sheets, but the rights to use and sell these players (under the rules of the respective association) its balance sheet as an intangible asset.

2.8   Accrual basis of accounting

The convention is that firms should prepare financial statements at least once in every calendar year. Where companies have a Stock Exchange listing they are required to produce an interim report six months into the accounting year, maybe even every quarter. Because firms undertake economic transactions on a continual basis, the arbitrary closing of accounting books at the end of a reporting period leads to a fundamental measurement problem, because for this one point in time in a year, companies have to prepare the financial statements to report the status at that point in time. Important questions will automatically come up, e.g.

- In which period exactly is revenue to be recognized in the income statement to increase Net Profit of the year?
- In which period exactly is the expense an expense?

Since Net Profit is the most important periodic performance metric under accrual accounting, the question concerning the period into which revenues and expenses belong, is not trivial at all.

Example 2-2: Accrual accounting

(1) If, during a year, a company **sells and delivers** €10m of goods, but collects only €8m from customers, it will show these sales as €10m in the income statement. The cash yet to be collected from customers is reported as an asset called Receivables in the balance statement.

(2) If, during the year, the company **uses** electricity costing €5m but has only paid €4m so far, it will show the expense of €5m in the income statement. The unpaid electricity bill is reported as a liability in the balance sheet.

(3) If, during a year, a company manufactures goods (i.e. buying materials, processing the materials, paying salaries, using machinery and equipment), but does not sell a single item made during the period, these cost will not be recognized in the income statement as expenses, and they will not lower Net Profit! Instead the items produced will show up in the balance sheet as finished goods or work in process. The example may be far fetched, but it illustrates a very important principle in the context of the matching principle.

Under the accruals basis, the effects of transactions and other events are recognized when they **occur** or are **realized** (and not when cash or its equivalent is received or paid!) and they are recorded in the accounting records and reported in the financial statements of the periods **to which they relate**.

Expenses, for instance, are *economic resources used up in a time period*. Expense recognition is not about when materials or salaries for personnel have been paid – but when have they been used up. So expense recognition is governed by the **matching principle**.

Matching has two forms, *matching losses or gains against time* and *matching expenses against revenue*.

- Time matching occurs when a gain or loss is spread over the relevant period of time, such as receiving interest on a loan or paying rent on a property.

- Matching of revenues and expenses occurs when costs such as labor are matched against the revenue earned from providing goods or services.

Example 2-3: Expense recognition – matching with revenues

In No. (3) of Example 2-2 the expense was **not** recognized in the period where the resources to manufacture the items have been **paid** – they will be recognized as expense in the period where the manufactured items are **sold**. Why? Because the moment the items have been sold is the moment in which the company actually loses the wealth of possessing these items! This is how accounting people think.

Though the company had to pay for the materials and the salaries and the machinery used to manufacture the products, the Sales revenues and Cost of Goods Sold (COGS) will appear in the **same** Income statement and they represent the monetary values for the identical physical quantity. So the *expenses are following the revenues* – one practical application of the matching principle.

2.9   Prudence

The prudence convention holds that caution should be exercised when making accounting judgments. Uncertainty about the future is dealt with by recording all losses at once and in full; this refers to both actual losses and expected losses. Profits, on the other hand, are recognized only when they actually arise. Profits and losses, or income and expenses – are treated differently. Income is generally recognized when *realized*; expenses are already recognized in the period in which they are *incurred*.

Generally, expected losses play an important role in reporting, whereas expected profits do not. To illustrate the application of this convention, let us assume that the company anticipates a certain future cost for warranties it has to provide to customers for products it has sold during the year. A company will therefore, as a matter of prudence, charge an amount against its profits equal to the amount it expects to lose by providing the repairs or replacements necessary to fulfill their future obligation. Such a charge is referred to as a *provision for warranties*.

Keep this very important point in mind: *a recognized provision has exactly the same effect as any expense, i.e., it reduces profit, hence it reduces equity – but a recognized provision does not represent a cash outflow. In addition to an ordinary expense a recognized provision produces a debt position in the balance sheet.* A company has to release a provision if it is no longer probable that an outflow of economic benefits will be required to settle the obligation. *A reversal of a provision has the same effect as adding an amount of extra income to the year's profits.*

While managers may properly recognize and measure those provisions, their use can also be perverted to manage earnings. Since the measurement of the provisions lies within the discretion of managers, provisions can be used to smooth out profits that are good in some years and poor in others. For example, a company can make excessive provisions in years when profits are high and reverse them in years when profits are low. While there is nothing criminal about such an act, we could argue that the use of this technique is deceptive and shareholders can be misled to some degree by this sort of accounting.

2.10 Revenue recognition

The revenue recognition principle indicates that revenue is to be recognized when it is probable that future economic benefits will flow to the company and reliable measurement of the amount of revenue is possible. Based on these fundamental concepts of revenue recognition, criteria are then established for various kinds of revenue transactions through the development of related IFRS. For example, there is a standard on revenue that identifies the circumstances in which revenue recognition criteria are met for various revenue transactions.

Generally, an objective test, such as a sale, indicates the point at which a company recognizes revenue. The **sale** – and not the cash received for the products or the service! – provides an objective and verifiable measure of revenue. Any basis for revenue recognition short of actual sale opens the door to wide variations in practice. Recognition at the time of sale provides a uniform and reasonable test. However, some exceptions to the rule exist.

- *Percentage-of-Completion Method* In IFRS, a company can eventually recognize revenue before it completes the job in certain long-term construction contracts. In this method, a company recognizes revenue periodically, based on the percentage of the job it has completed. Although technically a transfer of ownership has not occurred, it is probable that future economic benefits will flow to the company. If it is not possible to obtain dependable estimates of cost and progress, then company delays revenue recognition until it completes the job.

- *Completed-Contract Method* Other accounting standards only allow a company to recognize revenue after completion of the product and when full delivery as taken place. This makes it especially difficult for construction companies to actually recognize a revenue before a multi-year project has been finished.

Hence, *IAS 18* says that revenue should be recognized when:
- significant risks and rewards of ownership are transferred to the buyer;

- managerial involvement and control have passed;
- the amount of revenue can be measured reliably;
- it is probable that economic benefits will flow to the enterprise; and
- the costs of the transaction (including future costs) can be measured reliably.

The IASB and the FASB have issued new requirements for recognizing revenue under both IFRS and US GAAP. IFRS 15 *Revenue from Contracts with Customers* (which is presented and discussed on page 76 in section 4.4) provides a single revenue recognition model based on the transfer of control of a good or service to a customer. It will be effective on 1 January 2018, with early adoption only permitted under IFRS.

IFRS 15 marks a change from current requirements under IFRS (IAS 18 and others). It provides a more structured approach to measuring and recognizing revenue, with detailed application guidance. Therefore, adoption may be a significant undertaking for many entities.

2.11   Relevance vs. Reliability

The historic cost convention says that the value of assets shown on the balance sheet should be based on their acquisition cost (that is, historic cost). For accounting and finance people, the acquisition cost is a measurement of value *which is confirmed by a market transaction between two independent parties* – therefore we may argue that this way more **reliable information** is produced. Reporting in this way reduces the need for judgments, as the amount paid for a particular asset is usually a matter of **demonstrable fact**.

The drawback of this method is however that information based on past costs – though reliable – may not always be **relevant** to the needs of users. It could be argued that the historic cost convention is difficult to support, as outdated historic costs are unlikely to help in the assessment of the current financial position. Hence, recording assets at their current value would provide a more realistic view of financial position and would be relevant for a wide range of decisions. But there are some problems with any system of measurement based on current values, too.

So what's wrong with *current value* or *fair value* measurements? First, the term 'current value' can be defined in a number of different ways. For example, it can be defined broadly as either the current *replacement cost* or the current *realisable value* (which is something like a *hypothetical* selling price) of an asset. These two types of valuation may result in quite different figures being produced to represent the current value of an item. It would be similar to the price spread in secondhand car values: there is always a difference between buying and selling prices.

In addition, the terms *replacement cost* and *realisable value* are not as clearly defined as they sound – they can be defined in different ways. We must therefore be clear about what kind of current value accounting we wish to use. And since these terms are not so clearly defined, there is room for interpretation by those who prepare the financial statements – so it is difficult to determine values with any real degree of objectivity.

People who oppose fair value measurement argue that measurement based on fair value introduces *increased subjectivity into accounting reports*, when fair value information is not readily available. For example, it is easy to arrive at fair values when the assets in question are traded in liquid markets with many traders, but fair values are not readily available in other situations when there is no active market generating fair market prices. In these situations, companies may rely on *valuation models based on discounted expected cash flows* to arrive at fair value measurements. Obviously, a great deal of expertise and sound judgment is needed to arrive at measures that are representationally faithful. This may mean that the figures produced are heavily dependent on the opinion of managers which might affect the credibility among users of the financial statements.

2.12   Substance over form

The IFRS Framework describes substance over form as follows: "If information is to represent faithfully the transactions and other events that it purports to represent, it is necessary that they are accounted for and presented in accordance with their substance and economic reality and not merely their legal form. The substance of transactions or other events is not always consistent with that which is apparent from their legal or contrived form. For example, an entity may dispose of an asset to another party in such a way that the documentation purports to pass legal ownership to that party; nevertheless, agreements may exist that ensure that the entity continues to enjoy the future economic benefits embodied in the asset. In such circumstances, the reporting of a sale would not represent faithfully the transaction entered into (if indeed there was a transaction)."

The typical example is the lease contract, e.g. when a machine is leased for a five year period then handed back or purchased for some agreed amount of money. The legal form is that the machine is still **legally owned** by the lessor but the economic reality is that the company assumes the full responsibility for the machine – being the **economic owner** for the best part of the machine's economic life. So eventually – if certain criteria according to *IAS 17* are met – the machine should be recognized as a tangible fixed asset and a liability for the payments to the lessor recognized under current and long-term liabilities.

3   Elements of Financial Statements

3.1   Balance Sheet

According to *IAS 1 Presentation of Financial Statements*, the balance sheet (or the *"statement of financial position"* as the standards call it now) is a required component of an entity's financial statements. IFRS require the balance sheet to present information on the entity's assets, liabilities, and equities. IAS 1 does not require a specific format for the balance sheet. It should classify each section as current and noncurrent unless the liquidity presentation is more appropriate. However, there is no requirement that current items precede noncurrent items or vice versa. IAS 1 allows entities to use the liquidity presentation if it increases the reliability and relevance of the information. If the liquidity presentation is used, assets and liabilities must be reported in order of liquidity. IFRS requires one year of comparative financial information.

The line items to be included on the face of the statement of financial position are:
- property, plant and equipment
- investment property
- intangible assets
- financial assets (excluding amounts shown under (e), (h), and (i))
- investments accounted for using the equity method
- biological assets
- inventories
- trade and other receivables
- cash and cash equivalents
- assets held for sale
- trade and other payables
- provisions
- financial liabilities (excluding amounts shown under (k) and (l))
- current tax liabilities and current tax assets, as defined in IAS 12
- deferred tax liabilities and deferred tax assets, as defined in IAS 12
- liabilities included in disposal groups
- non-controlling interests, presented within equity
- issued capital and reserves attributable to owners of the parent.

Additional line items, headings and subtotals may be needed to fairly present the entity's financial position.

In the equity section, IAS 1 requires entities to disclose:
- numbers of shares authorized, issued and fully paid, and issued but not fully paid
- par value (or that shares do not have a par value)
- a reconciliation of the number of shares outstanding at the beginning and the end of the period
- description of rights, preferences, and restrictions
- treasury shares, including shares held by subsidiaries and associates
- shares reserved for issuance under options and contracts
- a description of the nature and purpose of each reserve within equity.

Authorized Share Capital

The maximum amount of share capital a company that common shareholders allowed company management to raise is called its authorized capital. Though this does not limit the number of shares a company may issue, it does put a ceiling on the total amount of money that can be raised by the sale of those shares.

"Issued but not fully paid"

Depending on applicable regulations, companies may issue stock to investors with the understanding the investors will pay at a later date on request of management. It is assumed that investors will provide the funds when called.

Treasury stock (shares)

A treasury stock is shares of stock which is bought back by the issuing company, reducing the amount of outstanding stock on the open market. There are several motivations for a company's management to buy back their own stock:
- Stock repurchases may be a tax efficient method to give cash to shareholders, instead of paying dividends.
- Companies may try to support their stock when they feel that their stock is undervalued on the stock market.
- Companies may use the stock for employee or management compensation plans.
- A stock repurchase may be used to protect the company against a takeover threat, reducing available stock in the market.

3.2   Income Statement Formats

IAS 1 states that "an entity shall present an analysis of expenses using a classification based on either the nature of expenses or their function within the entity, whichever provides information that is reliable and more relevant". The 4th EU directive (1978) also accepts both types of classification of expenses for the income statement. If expenses are presented *by function*, additional disclosure is required for the amount of depreciation, amortization and employee benefit expense.

For IFRS, there is no set format for the income statement, but there are six required elements:

- Revenue
- Finance costs
- Profit or loss from associates and joint ventures accounted for using the equity method
- Tax expense
- Discontinued operations
- Profit or loss (bottom line)

An additional difference to other accounting standards (like US GAAP or German GAAP) is that IFRS prohibits items from being presented as *Extraordinary* (defined for US and German GAAP as material transactions both unusual in nature and infrequent in occurrence) either on the face of the income statement or in the accompanying notes.

So an entity has to present its expenses in the income statement based **on function** or **on nature** whichever provides information that is reliable and more relevant. But what does that mean "*based on function*" or "*based on nature*"?

In general, there are two methods to classify expenses:

Table 3-1: Income Statement "by nature" or "by function"

"by nature" – by type of expenditure	*"by function" – by cost center type*
Expenses are aggregated in the income statement directly according to their character or nature (e.g., materials, transportation costs, and taxes other than income tax, salaries and social security expenses, depreciation).	Expenses are classified according to the purpose or the cost center in which they occur: - manufacturing/purchasing: cost of goods sold or cost of sales; - Administration: administrative expenses - Selling: selling and distribution expenses

Net sales	Net sales revenue
+ Other operating revenues	– Cost of goods sold (cost of sales)
+/– Change in inventories of merchandise	= Gross margin
+ Work performed by the enterprise and capitalized	– Commercial and distribution expenses
– Raw materials and consumables used	– Administrative expenses
– Purchases of merchandise	– Other operating expenses
– Labor and personnel expenses	= Operating income
– Depreciation expense	
– Other operating expenses	
= Operating income	

The distinction between 'by nature' and 'by function' classification of expenses only applies to expenses reported **above operating income**. What happens in practice is highly variable across countries.

- While the U.S. and Canada, for example, have adopted a 'by function' income statement format, certain countries (e.g., Italy) prefer the 'by nature' format, and several others (e.g., Germany, see § 275 German Commercial Code) leave the choice up to the firms themselves, though firms are not allowed to change the format from period to period.

- But even in a country where the situation seems extremely clear, as is the case for the U.S., there may be exceptions to the rule. For example, airline accounting in the U.S. is partly governed by the Uniform System of Accounts and Reports (USAR) issued by the U.S. Department of Transportation (DOT) (2002). Pursuant to DOT regulations, income statements are normally presented 'by nature' rather than 'by function'.

- In France, the 'by nature' format is the traditional method for individual company income statements. However, the new French consolidation regulations allow companies to choose between the 'by nature' and 'by function' models for their consolidated income statement.[1]

Each format of presentation emanates from a certain vision of the business model that financial statements are supposed to describe. Neither choice is intrinsically better. Each is coherent with a certain philosophy and communication approach.

Both Example 3-1 and Example 3-2 explain the distinction and characteristics of both formats. Learners should study these carefully, as these formats offer some irritating features.

---

[1] Ding, Y./Jeanjean, T./Stolowy, H. (2008): The impact of firms' internationalization on financial statement presentation: Some French evidence, in: Advances in Accounting, incorporating Advances in International Accounting 24, (2008) 145-156.

Example 3-1: Income Statement Format "by nature of expense"

German Muck AG has collected the following data for the last fiscal year.

Production quantity (period)	2400	units
Quantity sold (period)	1900	units
Sales price (net)	860	per unit
Total direct material cost (period)	60,000	Euro

The overhead has been differentiated between purpose (function) or cost centers (production, administration and selling) and type of expenses (material, labor, depreciation, other).

Overhead (in Euro)				
	Production	Admin	Selling	Total
Indirect material expenses	264,000	48,000	60,000	372,000
Indirect labor cost	125,000	85,000	136,000	346,000
Depreciation	45,000	18,000	34,000	97,000
other expenses	284,000	46,300	164,800	495,100
Totals	718,000	197,300	394,800	1,310,100

The table above shows the two perspectives of classification. As you can see, all cost or expenses can be classified as either to be of a certain **nature** or being incurred in a specific **cost center** or **operational segment**. But it is still the same cost data. Now let's prepare the operational part of the income statements.

Step 1: Determine the Cost of Goods Manufactured for 1 unit

Production quantity	2,400 units
Direct material cost (went directly into the product)	60,000€
Overhead *only for production* in the period	718,000€
=> (718,000+60,000)/2,400 = **324.16666€ ≈ 324.17**	

Result: Each item **manufactured** in the period has incurred cost of **324.17€.**

Step 2: Determine the production value (COGM) for the goods that have **not** been sold

Muck has manufactured 2,400 units in the period, but only 1,900 were sold. So 500 is the number of units added to the finished goods inventory. The company may have spent money to make these goods, but this money spent for the 500 **is not an expense**. It should not reduce profit of the period. But in an income statement "by nature of expense" **all** expenditures are recognized, which means that the income statement contains expenditures for the production of the 500 units, which actually shouldn't reduce the profit. Therefore, an additional position is necessary to correct or neutralize these expenses. This position that corrects or neutralizes the excess expenses is called **change in inventory** of finished goods or work in process. It acts as an *income*, in case the company *manufactured more than it sold*.

On the other hand, the **change in inventory** will be an *additional expense*, if the company *sold more than it manufactured*. If that happens, the company must have sold items *from the last periods*, which have not yet been recognized as an expense. These items are an expense when they have been *used or sold* to generate income.

In our case though, the change in inventory is 500 × 324.1666 = 162,083€.

The sales revenue is simply 1,900 × 860 = 1,634,000.

We take the other data from the cost overview and get:

Income Statement "by type of expense"	in €	Calculation
Net sales	1,634,000	= 1,900 × 860
+ Change in WIP and FG	162,083	= 500 × 324.1666
- Cost of materials	-432,000	=372,000+60,000 total cost of materials
- Personnel expenses	-346,000	total labor overhead from cost sheet
- Depreciation	-97,000	total depreciation from cost sheet
- Other expenses	-495,100	total other op. exp. from cost sheet
= Income from operations	425,983	

Example 3-2: Income Statement Format "by function"

The data is still the same as Example 3-1 on page 38.

In an Income statement by function we compare Sales revenue with the manufacturing cost of the **exact quantity that was sold** – hence the name "Cost of goods **sold**". The difference of net sales and COGS is the **Gross profit** – which measures the surplus attributable to the production activities.

Income Statement format "by function"	in €	Calculation
Net sales	1,634,000	=1900 × 860
- Cost of sales (COGS)	-615,917	=1900 × 324.1666
= Gross profit	1,018,083	
- Selling expenses	-394,800	only the selling overhead
- General & admin expenses	-197,300	only the admin overhead
= **Income from operations**	**425,983**	

3.3   Assets and Liabilities – Definition and Recognition

Some definitions of assets and liabilities are quite simple. The reason for making these definitions so simple is to make it easier for learners to understand. So we might read definitions like "Assets are what a company owns, liabilities are what a company owes." These definitions are – to say it nicely – not very helpful.

Why are these definitions not helpful?

- They are not helpful because they imply that "legal ownership" is what defines an asset – but that's not correct. In case of a "finance lease" an item not legally owned by the company is still included in the company's balance sheet.

- "Owns" sounds like it should be a *tangible* asset, something we can see and touch – but that is also not correct. There are *intangible* assets that cannot be touched – like licenses or patents or goodwill.

- It might also sound like an asset is something that can be taken away from the company – but that is also not correct. *Goodwill* is an asset that cannot be touched and it cannot be taken away, it is not separable (IFRS call it "separable", if an asset can be taken away separately as a single asset).

- And with assets like "Deferred tax assets" it really gets complicated – because deferred tax assets are just the **expectation** to pay less taxes in later years. It is not even a receivable, which is a legal claim on being paid by a third party. So a deferred tax asset is not even a legal claim – but it is still an asset in the IFRS context.

Of course, experienced accounting people know all these complexities, and therefore the IFRS framework uses definitions which are more complex and quite rigorous. So the framework says:

"Recognition is the process of incorporating in the balance sheet or income statement an item that meets the definition of an element and satisfies the criteria for recognition. It involves the depiction of the item in words and by a monetary amount and the inclusion of that amount in the balance sheet or income statement totals. Items that satisfy the recognition criteria should be recognized in the balance sheet or income statement. The failure to recognize such items is not rectified by disclosure of the accounting policies used nor by notes or explanatory material."

Be aware of the part that says "an item that meets the definition of an element and satisfies the criteria for recognition". So there are *two* requirements for an item to be in the balance sheet or in the income statement: (1) It has to meet the definition of an element, and (2) it has to satisfy the criteria of recognition.

Let's look at both of them, the definitions and the recognition criteria.

Definitions IFRS Framework	
Assets	**Liabilities**
"An asset is a resource controlled by the entity as a result of past events and from which future economic benefits are expected to flow to the entity."	"A liability is a present obligation of the entity arising from past events, the settlement of which is expected to result in an outflow from the entity of resources embodying economic benefits."

Asset definition	
Control	A balance sheet does not necessarily show what a company legally owns, but what it controls. Control means to obtain the economic benefits from the asset and to exclude others from these benefits. Of course the strongest form of control is the right of ownership. But from an accounting and finance perspective, it is more important if the item can be exclusively used by the entity and that the entity makes the ultimate decisions concerning the asset.
Past events	"The past event" the evidence that the entity has actually gained control over the asset. Typically an asset is generated by a transaction: a purchase, a sale, an acquisition, the signing of a contract, the performance of a service.

Future economic benefits	An asset is an item that somehow will generate cash for the entity. On the other hand, it might not be only cash what the asset comprises. A receivable for example is the consequence of selling a product or providing a service, and it generates future economic benefits in form of the cash.
expected to flow	There must be the expectation that the future benefit will flow. If this cannot be confirmed by the entity, it is not an asset. If the entity found out that the debtor of the receivable will not be able to pay it may have to derecognize the asset.

Liability definition	
present obligation	In order to recognize a liability there does not have to be an obligation that is due on demand but rather there has to be a present obligation. The obligation can be legal (by contract or by law) or a constructive. A constructive obligation arises if past practice creates a valid expectation on the part of a third party, for example, a retail store that has a long-standing policy of allowing customers to return merchandise within, say, a 30-day period. The entity "constructed" the obligation themselves by their behavior or past decisions so that third parties may expect to receive certain benefits.
Past events	"The past event" the evidence that the entity has actually incurred an obligation. Typically an obligation is entered into by a transaction: a purchase, a sale, an acquisition, the signing of a contract, the performance of a service.
outflow of future economic benefits	Cash would be the economic benefit transferable to settle most obligations, but the transfer of assets or services to settle an obligation could also qualify as economic benefits.

So **even if** a transaction meets the definition of an asset/liability, it will not be recorded on the balance sheet unless it meets the following two *recognition criteria*:

1. It is *probable* that any *future economic benefit* associated with the item *will flow to or from the enterprise*; and

2. The item's *cost or value can be measured with reliability*.

If these cannot be passed initially then the transactions must be written off directly to income. If one of the criteria is subsequently failed, then the asset/liability must then be removed or derecognized from the balance sheet. It is possible that the asset/liability will need to be measured where there is sufficient evidence that the amount has changed, and the new amount measured with sufficient reliability.

Based on these general criteria:

- An *asset* is recognized in the balance sheet when it is probable that the future economic benefits will flow to the enterprise and the asset has a cost or value that can be measured reliably.

- A *liability* is recognized in the balance sheet when it is probable that an outflow of resources embodying economic benefits will result from the settlement of a present obligation and the amount at which the settlement will take place can be measured reliably.

3.4 Measurement

The IASB Framework states:

"Measurement is the process of determining the monetary amounts at which the elements of the financial statements are to be recognized and carried in the balance sheet and income statement. This involves the selection of the particular basis of measurement."

So measurement involves *assigning monetary amounts* at which the elements of the financial statements are to be recognized and reported.

The Framework acknowledges that a variety of measurement bases are used today to different degrees and in varying combinations in financial statements, including:

- Historical cost
- Replacement cost
- Current cost
- Net realizable value
- Present value
- Value in use
- Fair value

1. *Historic cost.* Assets recorded at cash paid or the fair value of the consideration given at date of acquisition. Liabilities are recorded at the fair value of the consideration received in exchange for the obligation or the amount of cash expected to be paid to satisfy the liability, e.g. taxation.

2. *Replacement cost.* The current acquisition cost of a similar asset, new or used, or of an equivalent productive capacity or service potential

3. *Current cost.* Assets recorded at cash that would have to be paid to acquire the same or equivalent asset. Liabilities are carried at the undiscounted amount of cash required to settle the obligation.

4. *Net realizable value.* The estimated selling price in the ordinary course of business less the estimated costs of completion and the estimated costs necessary to make the

sale. Liabilities are carried at their settlement values, i.e. the undiscounted amounts of cash expected to be paid to satisfy the liabilities in normal course of business.

5. *Present value.* Present value it is not a measurement basis in itself. Rather, it is a framework principle that can be applied to estimate a number of the above measurements in certain circumstances. The present value formulation is very important because it captures how expected future cash flows and the time value of money and attendant risks enter into the valuation of assets and liabilities. Since the cash-equivalent expectations attribute of assets and liabilities is a primary focus of accounting measurement, the present value formulation provides a foundation for evaluating how this attribute may be incorporated within different measurement bases. Assets recorded at the present discounted value of future net cash inflows that the item is expected to generate in the normal course of business. Liabilities are carried at the present discounted value of the future net cash outflows that are expected to be required to settle the liabilities in the normal course of business.

6. *Value in use.* The present value of estimated future cash flows expected to arise from the continuing use of an asset and from its disposal at the end of its useful life. Based on its use in standards and practice, it seems generally to be presumed that the objective is to reflect the best estimates of future cash flows of the reporting entity's management. However, the value in use measurement basis seems often to be interpreted in terms of discounting these management estimates using rates that reflect current market assessments of the time value of money and risks commensurate with those of the asset.

7. *Fair value.* The amount for which an asset or liability could be exchanged between knowledgeable, willing parties in an arm's length transaction. It is well accepted that the objective of fair value measurement is to represent the market price of an asset or liability at the measurement date. If there is no observable market price at the measurement date for the asset or liability to be measured, the fair value objective is to estimate what the market price *would be if there were a market.*

3.5   Income and Expenses

Definitions			
Income		**Expenses**	
Income is increases in economic benefits during the accounting period in the form of inflows or enhancements of assets or decreases of liabilities that result in increases in equity, other than those relating to contributions from equity participants.		Expenses are decreases in economic benefits during the accounting period in the form of outflows or depletions of assets or incurrences of liabilities that result in decreases in equity, other than those relating to distributions to equity participants.	
revenue	*gains*	*Expenses that arise in the course of the ordinary activities*	*Losses*
Revenue arises in the course of the ordinary activities of an entity and is referred to by a variety of different names including sales, fees, interest, dividends, royalties and rent.	Gains represent other items that meet the definition of income and may or may not arise in the course of the ordinary activities of an entity. Gains represent increases in economic benefits and as such are no different in nature from revenue.	Include, for example, cost of sales, wages and depreciation. They usually take the form of an outflow or depletion of assets such as cash and cash equivalents, inventory, property, plant and equipment.	Losses represent other items that meet the definition of expenses and may or may not, arise in the course of the ordinary activities of the entity. Losses represent decreases in economic benefits and as such they are no different in nature from other expenses.

Recognition	
Income	**Expenses**
Income is recognized in the income statement when increase in future economic benefits related to an increase in an asset or a decrease of a liability has arisen that can be measured reliably. This means, in effect, that recognition of income occurs simultaneously with the recognition of increases in assets or decreases in liabilities (for example, the net increase in assets arising on a sale of goods or services or the decrease in liabilities arising from the waiver of a debt payable).	Expenses are recognized when decrease in future economic benefits related to a decrease in an asset or an increase of a liability has arisen that can be measured reliably. This means, in effect, that recognition of expenses occurs simultaneously with the recognition of an increase in liabilities or a decrease in assets (for example, the accrual of employee entitlements or the depreciation of equipment).

Revenue from the sale of goods is recognized when all the following conditions have been satisfied

- The entity has transferred to the buyer significant risks and rewards of ownership of the goods;
- The entity retains neither continuing managerial involvement to the degree usually associated with ownership nor effective control over the goods sold;
- The amount of revenue can be measured reliably;
- It is probable that economic benefits associated with the transaction will flow to the entity;
- Costs incurred or to be incurred in respect to the transaction can be measured reliably.

3.6   Comprehensive Income and Recycling

Under IFRS, since 2012 entities are required to present either a combined statement of comprehensive income (one-statement approach) or two separate statements—one for profit and loss and one for other comprehensive income (two-statement-approach). So income in IFRS is made up of two categories:

(1) The **profit-and-loss-statement** is the classical income statement which contains revenues and expenses.

(2) **Other comprehensive income (OCI)** is a statement that includes items which are not typical revenues or expenses.

So the following relationship applies:

Comprehensive income	=	Profit or loss (PL)	+	Other comprehensive income (OCI)

Other comprehensive income

For a short moment, the reader may regard OCI as "not real income". Obviously, this is a very simplistic notion, but it helps to understand why IFRS finds itself in this strange situation to define two different income categories. The notion of OCI as "not real income" and for PL to be "real income" is supported by the fact that *earnings per share* are taken from the PL to be calculated. So in order to measure the earnings per share, the items from PL are used – making it "real income".

Though OCI is "not real income", it is the result of an increase in value of assets. If the carrying value of assets is *increased* to their "fair values" (e.g. property or financial instruments are written up in their book values), the mechanical consequence from the logic of a balance sheet is that equity will also increase – so any increase or decrease in equity which does

NOT come from transaction with owners (capital injections or withdrawals) should show up in the income statement.

But the standardsetters or any knowledgeable accounting professional would feel uncomfortable to interpret a mere increase in asset values as a profit in the sense that it has been earned in the period, or that it is the consequence of successful operational activities or that it eventually may be distributable to shareholders. After all, it is just some sort of an unrealized gain (or loss) which increases or decreases equity.[2]

Therefore, OCI are those changes in the value of assets that change also equity – but are not shown as income or expenses in the income statement. It is required to present these increases in equity *separated* from earnings (retained earnings) in the equity section. Usually they are referred to as "other components of equity" or OCE. This is done to increase the transparency of these items as users can easily distinguish them from those items presented as part of PL.

Furthermore, since 2012, entities have to group together items within OCI on the basis of whether they will eventually be "recycled" to PL. This change is aimed to provide users with clarity about the nature of items presented as OCI and their future impact on the income statement.

---

[2] There are two other possible OCI items: "foreign currency translation adjustments on foreign subsidiaries" and "actuarial gains and losses arising on a defined benefit pension plan". Both change positions in assets or liabilities and as a consequence, in equity. So they are gains or losses, but they do not represent "earnings", but rather changes of market prices (like interest rates, exchange rates or stock prices).

Example 3-3: Statement of comprehensive income – Hugo Boss 2014

The net income is the result from PL and part of comprehensive income.

The OCI is grouped in those items which will be recycled...

...and the items which will not be recycled.

PL + OCI = Total comprehensive income

CONSOLIDATED STATEMENT OF COMPREHENSIVE INCOME

OF THE HUGO BOSS GROUP FOR THE PERIOD FROM JANUARY 1 TO DECEMBER 31, 2014

04|02 CONSOLIDATED STATEMENT OF COMPREHENSIVE INCOME (in EUR thousand)

	2014	2013
Net income	334,480	333,359
Items that will not be reclassified to profit or loss		
Remeasurements of defined benefit plans	(11,632)	651
Items to be reclassified subsequently to profit or loss		
Currency differences	31,634	(11,921)
Gains/losses from cash flow hedges	(1,587)	4,480
Other comprehensive income, net of tax	18,415	(6,810)
Total comprehensive income	352,895	326,549
Attributable to:		
Equity holders of the parent company	352,062	322,582
Non-controlling interests	833	3,967
Total comprehensive income	352,895	326,549

Recycling or Reclassification

The question may come up what will happen eventually to such a position in OCI (which still is shown in equity). If an item was previously classified as OCI (because it was considered "not real income"), but later realized in PL (reclassifying it to "real income") – we call such a procedure "recycling" or "reclassification".

Let's start with the following examples of items that IFRS either permits or requires to be presented as OCI:

- Foreign currency translation adjustments on foreign subsidiaries
- Changes in the fair value of available-for-sale financial assets
- Actuarial gains and losses arising on a defined benefit pension plan
- Revaluations of property, plant and equipment
- Changes in the fair value of a financial instrument in a cash flow hedge

Example 3-4: No recycling from revaluation of PPE

IAS 16 PPE is one example of a standard that prohibits gains and losses to be reclassified from equity to PL as a reclassification adjustment. Let us assume the company bought land at a cost of €10m which is treated in accordance with IAS 16 PPE.

If the land is subsequently revalued to €12m, then the gain of €2m is recognized in OCI and will be taken to OCE. When in a later period the asset is sold for €13m, IAS 16 PPE specifically requires that the profit on disposal recognized in the PL is €1m – i.e. the difference between the sale proceeds of €13m and the carrying value of €12m.

The previously recognized gain of €2m is not recycled/reclassified back to PL as part of the gain on disposal. However the €2m balance in the OCE reserve is now redundant as the asset has been sold and the profit is realized. Accordingly, there will be a transfer in the Statement of Changes in Equity, from the OCE of €2m into RE.

There is no obvious principle that describes the nature of items so that they are excluded from PL and included in OCI. But it seems that all the OCI items come from remeasurement as a result of movements in a price or valuation of assets or liabilities and not from transactions.

- Some of these items (such as foreign currency translation adjustments and changes in the fair value of available-for-sale financial assets) are recognized in OCI but are then reclassified to PL when the underlying item (that is, the foreign subsidiary or available-for-sale financial asset) is sold or realized.

- In other cases (such as actuarial gains and losses and revaluations of property, plant and equipment) there is no such recycling.

Another word to the purpose of OCI

What can we say is the purpose of OCI and its separation from earnings? Which gains and losses on re-measurement to fair value should be reported in earnings and which in OCI? Which items, if any, should be recycled?

Officially, the IASB suggested that the PL should provide the *primary source of information about the return an entity has made on its economic resources in a period*. Accordingly the PL should recognize the results of transactions, consumption and impairments of assets and fulfilment of liabilities in the period in which they occur. In addition the PL would also recognize changes in the cost of assets and liabilities as well as any gains or losses resulting from their initial recognition. The role of the OCI would then be *to support the PL*. Gains and losses would only be recognized in OCI if it made the PL more relevant.

From a pure accounting standpoint, the OCI is the logical consequence of fair value accounting and the fact that some IAS/IFRS allow *writing up* an asset to its fair value, though that increase in asset value has not been "earned" by the company. As said before, if an asset is written up in the balance sheet with a higher value, the equity also must increase – after all, that is what a balance sheet does – it balances. Traditionally, any increase in equity is either a contribution by owners (which naturally is not recognized in the income statement, as it is no profit) or an income shown in the income statement. Also traditionally, an income is "earned" or at least "realized". But now we have situations that increase asset values, therefore increase somehow equity, but the standardsetters feel uncomfortable treating these increases in asset values as "income". Therefore we need a second income statement that shows those increases in equity which are not real income. The OCI is the consequence of breaking up with traditional accounting principles of clean-surplus-accounting which has been seen quite critical by a number of renowned authors.[3]

PL also contains unrealized gains

An additional complication is the fact that not only realized gains are included in profit or loss (PL) but also unrealized gains. So we cannot just say unrealized gains and losses are only shown in OCI – because there are also unrealized items in PL.

Examples for unrealized gains either in OCI or in PL:

- OCI: Gains on the revaluation of land and buildings accounted for in accordance with IAS 16, Property Plant and Equipment (IAS 16 PPE), are recognized in OCI and accumulate in equity in Other Components of Equity (OCE).

- PL: Gains on the revaluation of land and buildings accounted for in accordance with IAS 40, Investment Properties, are recognized in PL and are part of the Retained Earnings (RE).

Example for unrealized gains and losses on the financial asset of equity investments:

- If these equity investments (assets) are designated in accordance with IFRS 9, Financial Instruments (IFRS 9), at inception as *Fair Value Through Other Comprehensive Income* (FVTOCI) then the gains and losses are recognized in OCI and accumulated in equity in OCE.

- Whereas if management decides not to make this election, then the investment will by default be designated and accounted for as *Fair Value Through Profit or Loss* (FVTPL) and the gains and losses are recognized in PL and become part of RE.

---

[3] These are just some examples: Barker, Richard (2010): On the definitions of income, expenses and profit in IFRS. In: Accounting in Europe 7 (2), S. 147–158. Devalle, Alain; Magarini, Riccardo (2012): Assessing the value relevance of total comprehensive income under IFRS: an empirical evidence from European stock exchanges. In: International Journal of Accounting, Auditing and Performance Evaluation 8 (1), S. 43–68. Penman, Stephen H. (2010): Financial forecasting, risk and valuation: Accounting for the future. In: Abacus 46 (2), S. 211–228. Pronobis, Paul; Zülch, Henning (2011): The predictive power of comprehensive income and its individual components under IFRS. In: Problems and Perspectives in Management (PPM), Forthcoming.

Table 3-2: Components of Comprehensive Income

Comprehensive Income
"The change in equity during a period resulting from transactions and other events, other than those changes resulting from transactions with owners in their capacity as owners."

1. PL (Profit & Loss)
Content: Reflecting primary activities or relating to main revenue-producing activities.
Function: - PL provides the primary source of information about the return an entity has made on its economic resources in a period. - The PL should recognize the results of transactions, consumption and impairments of assets and fulfilment of liabilities in the period in which they occur or incur. - The PL would also recognize changes in the cost of assets and liabilities as well as any gains or losses resulting from their initial recognition.

Realized or incurred	*Not realized*
- Revenue von sale of goods or services; - Expenses incurred to make sales of goods or services; - other overhead expenses; - interest and taxes; - gains/losses from sale of PPE.	- Gains on the revaluation of land and buildings accounted for in accordance with **IAS 40** *Investment Properties*, are recognized in PL and are part of the Retained Earnings (RE); - Financial Assets by default designated and accounted for as *Fair Value Through Profit or Loss (FVTPL):* gains and losses are recognized in PL and become part of RE.

Comprehensive Income	
2. Other comprehensive income	
Content: Non-primary activities, non-revenue-producing activities, or simply not required or permitted to show in PL.	
Function: to support the PL	
to be recycled	*no recycling to PL*
IAS 21 *The Effects of Changes in Foreign Exchange Rate: Exchange* differences on translation of foreign operations. They are recognized in OCI and accumulated in "other components of equity" (OCE). On the disposal of the subsidiary or associate, IAS 21 requires that the net cumulative balance of group exchange differences be reclassified from equity to P&L as a reclassification adjustment – i.e. the balance of the group exchange differences in OCE is transferred to PL to form part of the profit on disposal.	- IAS 16: Gains on the revaluation of land and buildings accounted are recognized in OCI and accumulate in equity in Other Components of Equity (OCE) - IAS 16 PPE **prohibits** gains and losses to be reclassified from equity to PL as a reclassification adjustment. - IAS 19: Remeasurement of defined benefit plans; actuarial gains (losses).
- IAS 39: Gains or losses due to changes in fair values of cash flow hedges. - IAS 39: Gains or losses on *Available for sale financial assets*. - Income tax on items that may be reclassified to profit or loss.	IFRS 9 Financial Instruments: Gains or losses due to changes in own credit risk (financial liabilities) designated at fair value. IFRS 9: Gains or losses on investments in equity instruments subsequently measured at fair value through OCI (FVTOCI) and accumulated in OCE.

3.7   Single and Group financial statements

A *group* in an accounting sense is a *parent plus all its subsidiaries*. A group usually comes into existence when a company acquires or forms one or more other companies so that it either owns or controls this company wholly or partially. There are several ways in which a group is formed, e.g.

- An existing company takes over one or more other companies (= purchases them from their former owners or shareholders).

- A company can be set up as a group from its inception if the owners or founders decide that a group structure would best help them to achieve their objectives.

- An existing company may decide to split up its operations and set them up as two or more separate companies, while retaining ownership in the new companies.

Consolidated financial statements are the financial statements of a group presented *as if* they were a single economic entity. In accounting, *consolidation* refers to the mechanical process of bringing together the financial records of two or more entities to form a single set of statements.

A parent company will show its investments in ownership control (its subsidiaries) under the heading "Financial Investments" – so we wouldn't see the assets, liabilities and equity of the subsidiaries – we would just see "Financial Investments" on the asset side of the parent company's individual balance sheet. Single company financial statements report the assets, liabilities, revenues, and expenses of the parent company only and therefore provide little insight into the activities of subsidiaries. And it wouldn't help to also look at all the subsidiaries single financial statements either, as they still contain all the inter-group business transactions – apart from the problems that come with different countries accounting practices and currencies.

Therefore, in addition to all the individual financial statements that the parent and all the subsidiaries have to prepare, the parent company has to prepare *additional* statements – the Consolidated Financial Statements. Consolidated financial statements have only the purpose to *inform* – these statements report the combined assets, liabilities, revenues, and expenses of the parent company *and* its subsidiaries *as if they were one entity*.

In the simplest case, when one company owns controlling interest (more than 50%) of the common stock of one or more other companies, the financial results of this group of companies are combined into a set of consolidated financial statements.

The objective of consolidated financial statements is to reflect in *one* set of financial statements the results of *all* companies owned or controlled by the *parent corporation*. In the consolidated balance sheet, minority interest is the amount of equity investment made by outside shareholders to consolidated subsidiaries that are not 100% owned by the parent. For example, if the parent owns 80% of the subsidiary, then the minority interest is the amount of financing provided by the outside shareholders who own the other 20% of the subsidiary.

This minority interest is reported as part of owners' equity, but it is clearly listed separately from the parent's owners' equity.

Non-controlling interest (minority interest)

Non-controlling interest refers to the ownership of a subsidiary with less than 50% interest. In consolidated statements, a company acquiring over 50% interest in a firm reports 100% of the subsidiary's income. Earnings attributed to the minority interest will be subtracted on the face of the financial statements to present net income attributed to the parent.

The consolidated balance sheet also shows 100% of all the subsidiaries assets and liabilities, even if the parent does not own 100% of the subsidiary. This is called *full consolidation*. It follows the idea that the parent company – though not legally owning 100% of the the subsidiary – still *controls* the assets of the subsidiaries with their majority share – so it should be shown in the financial statements of the parent. The non-controlling interest shows only in equity of the parent company's consolidated balance sheet – it reflects the *ownership* of minority shareholders. So readers of the consolidated statements can see the volume of what the parent company *controls*, and which part of that is *owned* by outside shareholders.

3.8   Statement of Cash Flows

According to IFRS, entities must present a statement of cash flows. According to IAS 7, entities should provide information about historical changes in cash and cash equivalents.

- *Cash* comprises cash on hand and demand deposits.
- *Cash equivalents* are short-term, highly liquid investments that are readily convertible to known amounts of cash and which are subject to an insignificant risk of change in value.

Cash flows are to be classified according to *operating, investing, or financing* activities.

What differentiates a cash flow statement from an income statement?

An income statement shows the changes in *equity* arising mainly from the revenue generating activities that result in income and expenses (right side of the balance sheet) with the net income being the difference between all income and all expenses, but the statement of cash flow shows the changes in cash (left side of the balance sheet). Some transaction change both cash and income – e.g. a sale made for cash. But some transactions change equity, but not cash – e.g. a depreciation, which – as we know reduces profit but not cash. The purchase of materials, production labor salaries, depreciation and production overhead will not be expensed (as long the product has not been sold!), but it may well be a cash outflow.

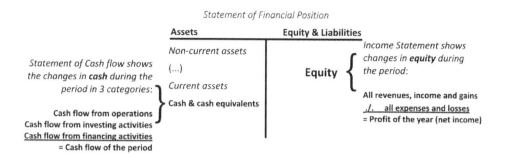

Keep in mind that profit (net income) is not cash. Naturally it is the profit of the company that increases the owner's wealth. But the company's well-being is dependent on its ability to generate cash – real money. Even profitable companies will eventually collapse if they do not have access to sufficient cash resources when needed. So it is very unlikely that the profit figure has any resemblance to the increase or decrease of the company's bank account.

The company's cash balance can be seen in the balance sheet. What we don't see is by which type of transactions the cash balance has increased or decreased over the year. This is what the statement of cash flows is for. It shows the major causes of change in the cash position and groups them into *operative cash flows*, *cash flow from investing* and *cash flow from financing*.

3.8.1   Components of Cash Flow

- *Cash flow from operating activities* results from the main revenue producing activities of the entity and other activities which are not investing or financing activities. These cash flows include taxes paid or received, unless they are clearly attributable to investing or financing activities.

- *Cash flow from investing activities* result from the acquisition and disposal of long-term assets and other investments that are not included in the cash equivalents.

- *Cash flow from financing activities* relate to changes to contributed equity and borrowings of an entity.

Generally, interest and dividends received or paid should be disclosed separately and can be classified as operating, investing or financing – but each item should be classified in a consistent manner from period to period as operating, investing or financing cash flows. IAS 7 requires entities to separately disclose interest and dividends received and paid. Entities also must separately disclose income taxes on the statement of cash flows.

3.8.2   Direct and indirect Method for the cash flow from operations

IFRS allows entities to use the direct or indirect method to prepare the statement of cash flows for report the cash flows from operating activities.

The direct method

The direct method shows operating cash receipts and payments, for example, cash paid to suppliers and employees and cash received from customers. This is useful to users as it shows the actual sources and uses of cash. However, many entities will not generate this information as a matter of course and so it may prove expensive to produce.

The indirect method

The indirect method instead starts with profit before taxation, adding back items shown elsewhere on the statement of cash flows (e.g. finance cost) and adjusting for non-cash items included in arriving at the operating profit figure. Non-cash items would include the following:

- *+Depreciation* This is a book adjustment to reflect the allocated cost of the asset; the cash impact of non-current assets is the buying of the asset.

- *– Profits/+ losses on disposal of non-current assets* If there was a profit on the disposal of non-current assets then the operating profit is too high by that amount and also the cash flow calculated would be too high, because this transaction is not "operations" but "investment" – so this profit will be subtracted. The cash generated by the disposal will consequentially appear in the *Cash flow from investment activities*. If the disposal of non-current assets produced a loss – the operational profit (and cash flow for that matter) is to be corrected by this loss. Just like a cash inflow, any cash outflow associated with the disposal is also reported in the Cash flow from investment activities.

- *Changes in inventories* As operating profit is calculated after charging cost of sales, which has been adjusted for opening and closing inventory we need the figure for total cash spent on materials in the year, not the cost of the goods used in the year. Any increase in inventories represents a use of cash, any decrease of inventories is a cash inflow.

- *Changes in receivables* The figure included in the profit or loss is the sales revenue – we need the cash received from customers and so we must take account of opening and closing receivables for the year.

- *Changes in payables* For the same reason as above – we need to get to the figure for actual cash paid to suppliers, but the direct method will occasionally be examined.

The concept behind the indirect method

The indirect method can be easily understood by looking at the balance sheet. The balance sheet shows values for the beginning of the year and for the end of the year – like a polaroid photograph of values. The *changes* to these static values are recorded both in the income statement and the cash flow statement.

- Any increase on the asset side of the balance sheet is a *use of cash*, and so is any decrease on the capital side of the balance sheet.

- Any decrease of the asset side is a *source of cash*, and so is any increase on the capital side of the balance sheet, like it is shown in the following table:

Table 3-3: Uses (–) and sources (+) of cash

Assets		Liabilities & Equity (Capital)	
Assets +	⇒ Cash –	Capital +	⇒ Cash +
Assets –	⇒ Cash +	Capital –	⇒ Cash –

Rearranging the balance sheet so that all increases in cash (= sources) and decreases in cash (=uses) are on the same side gives:

Uses of cash (–)	Sources of cash (+)
Assets + (other than cash)	Assets –
Capital –	Capital +

Example 3-5: Transactions and Cash flow components

Transactions or changes in the balance sheet...	...and their cumulated effect on cash flow (Cash + = Source of cash; Cash – = Use of cash)	Cash flow component
Net income (Capital +)	Cash +	Operative cash flow
Net loss (Capital –)	Cash –	Operative cash flow
Inventory increase	Cash –	Operative cash flow
Inventory decrease	Cash +	Operative cash flow
Receivable increase	Cash –	Operative cash flow
Receivable decrease	Cash +	Operative cash flow
Inventory increase	Cash –	Operative cash flow
Inventory decrease	Cash +	Operative cash flow
Trade payables decrease	Cash –	Operative cash flow
Trade payables increase	Cash +	Operative cash flow
Depreciation/Amortization	Cash +	Operative cash flow
Impairment	Cash +	Operative cash flow
Buying new fixed assets	Cash –	Investment cash flow
Disposal of fixed assets	Cash +	Investment cash flow
Acquisition of company	Cash –	Investment cash flow

Selling of company	Cash +	Investment cash flow
Lending funds (for interest)	Cash −	Investment cash flow
Taking a loan/issue bond	Cash +	Finance cash flow
Repaying debt	Cash −	Finance cash flow
Issuing new stock	Cash +	Finance cash flow
Paying dividends	Cash −	Finance cash flow

Example 3-6: Cash flow statement – Indirect Method

Muck AG has the prepared a statement of financial position and an income statement. The Statement of Cash flows has been prepared using the indirect method. The gain from disposal of PPE (60) refers to assets with a carrying value of 40 (which implies they were sold for 100).

	31.12.14	31.12.15		31.12.14	31.12.15
ASSETS			LIABILITIES		
Cash and equivalents	35,00	96,00	Accounts payable	120,00	130,00
Accounts Receivable	75,00	85,00	Notes payable	24,00	34,00
Inventories	140,00	130,00	Current portion long-term debt	50,00	40,00
Total Current Assets	250,00	317,00	Total Current Liabilities	194,00	204,00
PP&E	200,00	300,00	Long-term debt	210,00	250,00
Goodwill & Intangibles	30,00	25,00	Deferred taxes	44,00	53,00
Deferred Taxes	12,00	35,00	Total Non-Current Liabilities	254,00	303,00
Other Long Term Assets	125,00	145,00	Total Liabilities	448,00	507,00
Total Non-Current Assets	367,00	505,00			
			Shareholder's equity		
			Issued Stock	19,00	23,00
			Additional paid-in-capital	146,00	165,00
			Treasury Stock	-112,00	-132,00
			Retained Earnings	116,00	253,00
Total Assets	617,00	816,00	Total liabilities and SE	617,00	816,00

Income Statement	1/1/15-31/12/15
Net Revenues	895,00
-Cost of Goods Sold (COGS)	430,00
-Selling, general, & Administrative	125,00
-Research and development	60,00
-Depreciation	15,00
-Amortization	5,00
-Other operating expenses	15,00
+Gain from disposal of PPE	60,00
-Net Interest expense	45,00
=Pretax income	260,00
-Income tax expense (35%)	91,00
Profit of the year	169,00
Dividends	32,00

Cash Flow Statement	1/1/15-31/12/15	Comments
Net Income	169,00	directly from income statement
Depreciation and amortization	20,00	non-cash expense, added back to net income
Gain/loss from disposal of PPE	-60,00	PPE is "investment", so this income is subtracted here
Changes in working capital		
Accounts Receivable	-10,00	increase in assets => cash outflow
Inventories	10,00	decrease in assets => cash inflow
Accounts payable	10,00	increase in liabilities => cash inflow
Deferred taxes	-14,00	includes all changes in deferred taxes
Cash flow from operations	**125,00**	
Capital expenditures	-155,00	Increase in PPE (300-200) is a cash outflow, corrected for the depreciation (+15) and the carrying value of disposed assets (+40).
Cash from disposal of assets	100,00	Cash inflow from selling PPE (this is not the profit from the sale)
Long-term assets (ex. Deferred taxes)	-20,00	
Cash flow from investing	**-75,00**	
Increase in bank loan	10,00	increase in liabilities => cash inflow
Increase in long term debt	30,00	increase in liabilities => cash inflow
Increase in issued stock	4,00	increase in equity => cash inflow
Increase in additional paid in capital	19,00	increase in equity => cash inflow
Increase in Treasury stock	-20,00	Treasury stock are stocks bought back by the company. An increase is therefore a cash outflow.
Dividends	-32,00	decrease in equity
Cash from flow financing	**11,00**	
Beginning cash balance (12/2004)	35,00	
Total change in cash	61,00	
Ending cash balance (12/2005)	96,00	The ending cash balance calculated in the cash flow statement is the same figure as in the balance sheet.

We see from the cash flow statement that the company generated enough cash with its operations (+125) to pay for its investments (-75). So 50 was free to be used for debt or equity investors. Nevertheless, the company generated in total additional cash from its investors (+11), so that the total change in cash in the period was +61.

Example 3-7: Consolidated Statement of Cash Flows Hugo Boss Group 2014

04|05 CONSOLIDATED STATEMENT OF CASH FLOWS (in EUR thousand)

	Notes	2014	2013
	(35)		
Net income		334,480	333,359
Depreciation/amortization	(10)	122,760	105,262
Unrealized net foreign exchange gain/loss		(3,049)	18,916
Other non-cash transactions		5,178	(3,965)
Income tax expense/refund	(7)	102,668	100,107
Interest income and expenses	(6)	4,518	14,428
Change in inventories		(45,778)	(36,307)
Change in receivables and other assets		(31,987)	(30,584)
Change in trade payables and other liabilities		27,684	21,988
Result from disposal of non-current assets		(2,478)	2,741
Change in provisions for pensions	(26)	(1,319)	(2,414)
Change in other provisions		13,969	5,628
Income taxes paid		(128,389)	(104,799)
Cash flow from operations		**398,257**	**424,360**
Interest paid	(6)	(4,458)	(10,005)
Interest received	(6)	1,628	1,984
Cash flow from operating activities		**395,427**	**416,339**
Investments in property, plant and equipment	(12)	(104,459)	(160,243)
Investments in intangible assets	(11)	(25,307)	(13,083)
Acquisition of subsidiaries and other business entities less cash and cash equivalents acquired	(35)	0	(11,659)
Effects from disposal of subsidiaries		0	(1,698)
Cash receipts from sales of property, plant and equipment and intangible assets		2,702	366
Cash flow from investing activities		**(127,064)**	**(186,317)**
Dividends paid to equity holders of the parent company	(24)	(230,514)	(215,330)
Dividends paid to non-controlling interests		0	(2,448)
Change in current financial liabilities		262	(254,645)
Cash receipts from non-current financial liabilities		0	111,350
Repayment of non-current financial liabilities		(10,354)	0
Repayment of borrowings		(2,093)	(2,012)
Cash outflows for the purchase of additional interests in subsidiaries without change of control		(18,838)	0
Cash flow from financing activities		**(261,537)**	**(363,085)**
Exchange-rate related changes in cash and cash equivalents		2,563	(2,301)
Change in cash and cash equivalents		**9,389**	**(135,364)**
Cash and cash equivalents at the beginning of the period		119,242	254,606
Cash and cash equivalents at the end of the period	(18)	**128,631**	**119,242**

4   Assets

4.1   Property, Plant and Equipment (IAS 16)

IFRS defines property, plant, and equipment assets (abbreviated often as PPE) to be tangible, long-term in nature, and acquired for specific uses within the entity. IFRS does not include assets that are held for sale in the category of property, plant, and equipment.

Initial Recognition

IFRS recognizes PPE *if future economic benefits attributable to the asset are probable and it is possible to reliably measure the cost of the asset*. IFRS initially measures property, plant, and equipment *at cost*. The cost to acquire the asset includes *all costs incurred to bring the asset to the location and condition for its intended use*. This *includes* the cost of dismantling and removing the asset and restoring the site. The standard *prohibits* entities from capitalizing start-up costs, general administrative and overhead costs, or regular maintenance.

Capitalization of Interest in PPE

IAS 23 Borrowing Costs considers exchange rate differences from foreign currency borrowings an eligible borrowing cost. IFRS allows entities to offset borrowing costs by investment income earned on those borrowings. Under IFRS *the actual borrowing costs are capitalized*, so entities are required to capitalize borrowing costs related to the acquisition, construction or production of a qualifying asset.

Subsequent Costs

IFRS capitalize subsequent expenditures when it is probable that it will give rise to future economic benefits.

Subsequent Recognition

According to IAS 16 Property, Plant and Equipment, entities can follow the **cost model** or the **revaluation model**.

Subsequent Recognition IAS 16	
Cost Model	**Revaluation Model**
The cost model carries an item of property, plant and equipment at its cost less any accumulated depreciation and any accumulated impairment losses.	The revaluation model carries an item of property, plant and equipment at a **revalued amount**, which is its *fair value at the date of the revaluation less any subsequent accumulated depreciation and subsequent accumulated impairment losses.*
Reporting PPE **at cost** is the *benchmark* treatment but revaluation is a permitted alternative.	

Initial Revaluation

The revaluation model *revalues* property, plant, and equipment to its *fair value*. PPE is carried on the balance sheet at its fair value less accumulated depreciation (revalued) and any impairment losses. In order to qualify for the revaluation treatment, an *entire class* (e.g. land, buildings, vehicles, etc.) of property, plant, and equipment must be revalued. To account for a revaluation increase, a credit is made to equity as a revaluation surplus and a debit is made to the asset account. To account for a revaluation decrease, a credit is made to the asset account and a debit is made to an expense account.

Subsequent Revaluation of PPE

Subsequent decreases in value of an asset should first be charged against any previous revaluation surplus in respect to that asset, and the excess should be expensed. Note that revaluation surplus is nothing more than an increase in market or fair values of PPE – it is not earned like revenue. Therefore any *decreases* in value in following years have to "eat up" the previous increases. Only after these previous revaluation increases in market or fair values have been erased, any decreases in value result in *expenses* which show up in PL reducing profit.

If previous revaluations resulted in an expense, subsequent increases in value should be charged to income to the extent of the previous expense. The excess should be credited to equity. Once an asset has been revalued, its value on the balance sheet must represent its current fair value. At each year end, management should consider whether the asset's fair value differs from its carrying value. The carrying value should not differ materially from the asset's fair value.

Example 4-1 Revaluation of PPE

During the current year, German Muck AG decided to measure property, plant, and equipment at revalued amounts. Assume Muck AG owns a building with a cost of 190,000€ and a current fair value of 200,000€.

The journal entry to increase the carrying amount of the building to its fair value is

Debit record	Credit record
Buildings 10,000€	Revaluation surplus (Buildings) 10,000€

Note that *Revaluation surplus* is a position in *equity* so that the balance sheet totals *increase on both sides of the balance sheet*. But the increase in equity does not show in the income statement – so the revaluation to the upside does not increase profit.

In the following year, Muck AG determines that the fair value of the building is no longer 200,000€. Assuming the fair value has decreased to 160,000€, the following entry should be made:

Debit record	Credit record
Loss on buildings (expense) 30,000€	Buildings 40,000€
Revaluation surplus (Building) 10,000€	

Treatment of Accumulated Depreciation on Revaluation

Accumulated depreciation must be revalued. The following two methods are permitted.

(1) Accumulated depreciation is restated proportionately with the change in the gross carrying amount of the revalued asset. The carrying amount of the asset after revaluation should equal its revalued amount.

(2) Accumulated depreciation is eliminated against the gross carrying amount of the asset and the net amount is restated to the revalued amount of the asset.

What is a contra asset account?

Contra asset accounts are accounts used to adjust (reduce) the amounts associated with specific asset accounts.

The *first contra asset account is the accumulated depreciation account*. It belongs to an asset account like Property, Plant & Equipment (Fixed assets) and shows the amount by which the gross amount (historical cost = whatever the company paid to get these assets when they acquired them) is reduced to show all annual depreciation until now. Increases in contra asset accounts mean larger subtractions from the historical cost of these assets.

When a non-current-term asset, such as a building, is acquired for cash the building asset account is debited and the cash account is credited. As the building ages depreciation expense is reported in the income statement. The entry is a debit to depreciation expense and a credit to accumulated depreciation. Now the company can show in the balance sheet both the gross value (original cost) of the building and the net value (original cost less accumulated depreciation) of the building.

The mechanics of a contra asset account are identical to the mechanics of a liability account. Whatever reduces the assets is a credit entry, hence the increase of the accumulated depreciation account is a credit entry. The annual depreciation is also an expense in the income statement. Whatever reduces the right side of the balance sheet (an expense reduces equity) results in a debit entry.

The *second contra asset account is the 'estimated bad debts' account*.

When a company makes credit sales it *debits* accounts receivable (=increase of an asset) and *credits* sales revenue (=increase in equity). However, because the company expects that some purchasers will default on their debt it will have to estimate the amount that will not be paid. The estimated amount will be treated by *debiting* bad debt expense (or provision for bad debts) and *crediting* the estimated bad debts account. Then the company can see its gross accounts receivable and net accounts receivable (accounts receivable less estimated bad debts).

Some customers will actually default on the debt. The accounts receivable account is then credited (=reduced) and the 'estimated bad debts' account is debited (=also reduced, because now it is no longer an estimation, but certainty) when this happens. This means that this particular receivable is written off and the 'estimated bad debts' contra asset account falls. After all, the particular bad debt is no longer 'estimated'. It has now been realized.

Accumulated depreciation as a contra asset account

Accumulated depreciation is a contra asset account that adjusts the book value of the capital assets. It is written on the asset side of the balance sheet, and it can be interpreted as a *negative* asset position, as it *reduces* the gross value of the asset in the balance sheet. So if a fixed asset was purchased for 100,000€ has 30,000€ of accumulated depreciation, the carrying value of this asset would be 70,000€. It would be shown in the balance sheet like this:

Assets		Liabilities and Equity
PPE (at cost)	100,000	[...]
./. accu. depr.	30,000	
Carrying value PPE	70,000	

Each year as the accumulated depreciation *increases*, the carrying value of the fixed asset *decreases* until the book value is zero. So if in the current year the period depreciation is 10,000€, the accumulated depreciation account would increase by 10,000. The accumulated depreciation journal entry is recorded by debiting the depreciation expense account and crediting the accumulated depreciation account:

Debit record	Credit record
Depreciation expense 10,000€	Accumulated Depreciation 10,000€

Example 4-2: Accumulated Depreciation

Muck AG owns a building that cost 800,000€. The building has accumulated depreciation of 200,000€ so the carrying value is 600,000€. Assume Muck AG revalues the building to its current fair value of 1,000,000€. All journal entries will not consider the impact on deferred taxes.

Treatment 1

Under treatment 1, Muck would restate the building account and the accumulated depreciation account such that the ratio of net carrying amount to gross carrying amount is 75% (600,000/800,000). This looks like as if the "new" *gross* carrying of the building (its cost) is now 1,333,333 – but this is only because the new *net* carrying amount is 1 million, which should also represent 75 percent after accumulated depreciation. The method pretends as if 25 percent has been depreciated consistently for all valuations.

before revaluation		percent	after revaluation		percent
Building (at cost)	800,000	100	Building (at cost)	1,333,333	100
less: acc. depreciation	(200,000)	25	less: acc. depreciation	(333,333)	25
Carrying value (net book value)	600,000	75	Carrying value (net book value)	1,000,000	75

Accordingly, the new accumulated depreciation is 333,333€. The accumulated depreciation account contains already the 200,000 – which means an additional 133,333 has to be added to the account. In the same manner, the Building at cost account is now increased by 533,333:

Debit record	Credit record
Buildings (cost) 533,333€	Accumulated Depreciation 133,333€
	Revaluation Surplus 400,000€

The revaluation surplus is 400,000€ - the increase in the net book value of the asset. This increase is credited to the revaluation surplus and it is shown only in Other Comprehensive Income.

Treatment 2

Muck AG would simply *eliminate* accumulated depreciation of 200,000€, so that only the net book value (carrying value) of 600,000€ remains in the balance sheet. Then the buildings account is increased by 400,000€ – and so is the revaluation surplus.

Debit record	Credit record
Accumulated depreciation 200,000€	Buildings 200,000€
Buildings 400,000€	Revaluation Surplus 400,000€

Example 4-3 Cost Model and Revaluation Model

At the beginning of 2010, Muck AG has purchased a fixed asset has for 3,500,000€. For the purpose of measurement subsequent to initial recognition it cannot be separated in components. Useful life is 7 years and no residual value is expected. Muck uses a straight-line depreciation to allocate cost over useful life. A revaluation is to be carried out every two years.

Year End	Cost less accumulated depreciation (in T-€)	fair value less cost to sell	value in use
2010	3000	2800	2700
2011	2500	2450	2400
2012	2000	2400	2580
2013	1500	1850	1950
2014	1000	950	950
2015	500	450	500
2016	0	0	0

Important aspects of the basic procedure

Impairment

- Assess at each balance sheet date whether there is any *indication* that an asset may be impaired (i.e. its recoverable amount is lower than its carrying amount). If there is an indication that an asset may be impaired, then the asset's *recoverable amount* must be calculated.

- Recoverable amount is the *higher* of an asset's fair value less costs to sell and its value in use.

- An impairment loss is recognized whenever recoverable amount is below carrying amount.

- The impairment loss is recognized as an *expense* (unless it relates to a revalued asset where the impairment loss is treated as a revaluation decrease).

Reversal of impairment

- Assess at each balance sheet date whether there is an indication that an impairment loss may have **decreased**. If so, calculate recoverable amount.

- The increased carrying amount due to a *reversal should not be more than what the depreciated historical cost would have been if the impairment had not been recognized*. So there is an upper limit for the carrying amount after a reversal of a previous impairment. Reversal of an impairment loss is recognized in the profit or loss (unless it relates to a revalued asset).

Revaluation (only when using the revaluation model)

- The asset is carried at a revalued amount, being its *fair value* at the date of revaluation less subsequent depreciation and impairment, provided that fair value can be measured reliably. This means, if a company uses the revaluation model, the revalued amount will always be the **fair value** (not the recoverable amount, not the value in use).

- If a revaluation results in an increase in value, it should be credited to *other comprehensive income* and *accumulated in equity under the heading "revaluation surplus"* unless it represents the reversal of a revaluation decrease of the same asset previously recognized as an expense, in which case it should be recognized in profit or loss.

- A decrease arising as a result of a revaluation should be recognized as an expense to the extent that it exceeds any amount previously credited to the revaluation surplus relating to the same asset.

- When a revalued asset is disposed of, any revaluation surplus may be transferred directly to retained earnings, or it may be left in equity under the heading revaluation surplus. The transfer to retained earnings should not be made through profit or loss.

Subsequent measurement: Cost Model

(CV = carrying value)

Year end	CV beginning of year (1)	depreciation	CV − depr. (2)	recov. amount (3)	Impairment (4)	Reversal of impairment (5)	CV end of year (6)
2010	3500	500	3000	2800	200	0	2800
2011	2800	467	2333	2450	0	117	2450
2012	2450	490	1960	2580	0	40	2000
2013	2000	500	1500	1950	0	0	1500
2014	1500	500	1000	950	50	0	950
2015	950	475	475	500	0	25	500
2016	500	500	0	0	0	0	0

"An impairment loss is recognized whenever recoverable amount is below carrying amount."

- But this means, that the annual depreciation has first to be subtracted from the carrying amount at the beginning of the year (2). Then recoverable amount (3) is compared to the carrying amount (2). If (3) is lower than (2), then the difference is the impairment (4).
- This happens in year 2010 and 2014.
- The depreciation is always calculated based on the carrying value at the end of the year (6) for the remaining number of years.

"The increased carrying amount due to a reversal should not be more than what the depreciated historical cost would have been if the impairment had not been recognized."

- The "depreciated historical cost" is the original depreciation schedule if no impairments had happened. These depreciated historical cost are the upper limit for any reversals. So if impairment is reversed, we have to check for the upper limit – even if the recoverable amount is higher, it won't be considered.
- This situation happens in 2012. The recoverable amount is 2580, and the current CV (2) is 1960. So obviously too much has been impaired in the previous years – this needs to be reversed, but only up to 2000, which is what the historical cost minus depreciation would have been originally without any impairments. In a way of speaking, at the end of 2012, the company is "back on track" with its original depreciation schedule – hence the next annual depreciation is 500. A similar situation happens in 2015, where the reversal is done up to 500.

Subsequent measurement Revaluation Model

(CV = carrying value)

Year end	CV beginning of year (1)	depreciation	CV – depr. (2)	recoverable amount or revalued amount (rev) (3)	Impairment (4)	Reversal of impairment (5)	Reval. surplus (OCE)	CV end of year (6)
2010	3.500	500	3.000	2800	200	0		2.800
2011	2.800	467	2.333	2450 (rev)	0	117		2.450
2012	2.450	490	1.960	2580	0	40		2.000
2013	2.000	500	1.500	1850 (rev.)	0	43	307	1.850
2014	1.850	617	1.233	950	[283 no expense]	0	-283	950
2015	950	475	475	450 (rev.	1 expense	0	-24	450
2016	450	450	0	0	0	0		0

Year end	Comments
2010	Recoverable amount is 2,800 – so the asset has to be impaired by 200 from 3,000.
2011	New carrying value of 2,800 is depreciated for the remaining 6 years (2,800/6=467), with carrying value after depreciation of 2,333. 2011 is a revaluation year, so the fair value of 2,450 will be the new carrying value. The impairment of 200 from 2010 is partially reversed with 117.
2012	The carrying value of 2,450 is depreciated for 5 years (=2,450/5 =490) to 1960. Recoverable amount is 2,580, so any remaining impairment has to be reversed – but not higher than the historical cost minus accumulated depreciation if no impairment had happened, which is 2,000. So 2,000 is the new carrying value at the end of 2012.
2013	2013 is a revaluation year, so 1,850 is the new carrying value, which is higher than the 1,500. So revaluation is 350. But not all of the 350 is OCI, because there is some previous impairment to reverse. Total impairment was 200, of which 117 and 40 was reversed in previous years. Now the remaining 43 will be reversed, and the remaining revaluation is 307, which will be shown in OCI.
2014	1,850/3=617 (annual depreciation) => carrying value is 1,233. Recoverable amount is 950, which leads to an impairment of 283, so that the revaluation surplus is "eaten up" first. Remaining revaluation surplus is 307-283=24.
2015	2015 is a revaluation year, and the fair value is 450. 25 have to be impaired, of which 24 reduce the remaining revaluation surplus. The remaining 1 will be expensed.
2016	450 will be depreciated. The asset is now fully depreciated.

4.2   Investment Property (IAS 40)

IFRS differentiates between property used for operational reasons and property (land or a building or part of a building or both) held (by the owner or by the lessee under a finance lease) to earn rentals or for capital appreciation or both.

- Investment property includes:
- Land held for long-term capital appreciation
- Land held for indeterminate future use
- Building leased out under an operating lease
- Vacant building held to be leased out under an operating lease
- Property being constructed/developed for future use as investment property.

Table 4-1: Transactions for which IAS 40 is not to be applied

IAS 40 is not to be applied for	Standard to be applied
Property held for use in the production or supply of goods or services or for administrative purposes	IAS 16 PPE
Property held for sale in the ordinary course of business or in the process of construction or development for such sale	IAS 2 Inventories
Property being constructed or developed on behalf of third parties	IAS 11 Construction Contracts
Owner-occupied property	IAS 16 PPE
Property leased to another entity under a finance lease	IAS 17 Leases

Initial recognition and measurement

Investment property is recognized as an asset when it is probable that the future economic benefits that are associated with the property will flow to the enterprise, and the cost of the property can be reliably measured.

Investment property is initially measured at cost, including transaction costs. Cost does not include start-up costs, abnormal waste, or initial operating losses incurred before the investment property achieves the planned level of occupancy.

Subsequent Measurement

An entity can *choose* between the fair value and the cost model. The accounting policy choice must be applied to all investment property.

Fair value model

- Investment properties are measured at *fair value*, which is the price that would be received to sell the investment property in an orderly transaction between market participants at the measurement date.
- Gains or losses arising from changes in the fair value of investment property *must be included in profit or loss for the period in which it arises.*
- In rare exceptional circumstances if fair value cannot be determined, the cost model in IAS 16 is used to measure the investment property.

Cost model

Investment property is measured in accordance with requirements set out for that model in IAS 16.

4.3   Intangible Assets (IAS 38)

Assets don't have to be physical, tangible items like land, buildings or machinery. Looking at the asset definition, it says that an asset is a resource, controlled by the enterprise, as a result of past events, and from which future benefits are expected to flow to the enterprise. It doesn't say that an asset has to have a physical substance.

Intangible Assets are identifiable, non-monetary assets without physical substance. "Identifiable" means they are either

- capable of being separated and sold, licensed, rented, transferred, exchanged or rented separately, or
- they arise from contractual or other legal rights.

From an accounting standpoint, the company may get such intangible assets in various ways:

- from a separate acquisition, which means the company just purchased them;
- the company may have acquired such intangible assets in a business combination (by acquiring other companies);
- they may be internally generated;
- they might be exchanged for some other asset (so instead of paying with money, the company exchanged it for something else but not money);

- certain rights could be granted by the government (e.g. license to operate a lottery, taxi licenses etc.).

The question is how to handle the recognition and the measurement. Do such transactions qualify to be recognized in the financial statements, and if so, with what values?

Particularly complicated are the *internally generated intangible assets*. Why is this? Accounting people don't like the idea that assets find their way into the balance sheet if they were not acquired in arm's length market transactions so that these assets can be measured reliably. But companies may spend a lot of money for research and development of new products, which may or may not generate revenues in future periods. Car manufacturers and pharmaceutical companies will often invest billions in new products, with years ahead until these products are marketable – if at all. Typically these expenditures cover items like salaries for engineers or materials which would normally qualify as expenses only – so spending money for these items reduces profit in these periods.

- From a practical business standpoint one may argue that managers might not like the idea to generate huge expenses in **this** period for eventual profits of the **later** periods thereby reducing their profit-linked compensation. Expensing all those development cost may create an incentive for a management behavior we call *underinvesting*.

- From a theoretical accounting standpoint one may argue that these expenditures are not really *period expenses*, but rather investments in the future. So they do not follow the matching principle, whereby expenses should follow the revenues they help to produce in the period. But since this money spent does not create assets by definition, no assets would appear in the balance sheet.

IAS 38 tries to solve this dilemma by defining quite strong criteria so that specific development expenses qualify as an **asset** so that those expenditures do **not** reduce profit of the period.

Initial Recognition

Intangible assets with *finite lives* are typically carried at *historical cost less accumulated amortization and impairment*. Intangible assets with *indefinite lives* (no foreseeable limit to their benefit) are not amortized, but are carried at historical cost less impairment.

IAS 38 Intangible Assets allows an alternative method of carrying intangible assets with finite lives. If a price is available on an active market (actually a condition rarely met in practice), the asset may be carried at fair value less accumulated amortization and impairment. Examples of intangible assets that may be priced on an active market include taxi licenses, fishing licenses, and production quotas. If the company chooses the alternative *revaluation method*, the asset fair value should be assessed regularly, typically annually. An increase in fair value of the asset is credited to the equity account *revaluation surplus*, except to the extent it reverses a previously recorded decrease reported directly in profit and loss.

A decrease in fair value is debited to the revaluation surplus account, until the account surplus for the specific asset is reduced to zero. Any remaining decrease is recognized in profit and loss.

Research and development cost

Another type of intangible assets is **internally generated intangibles**. For IFRS, the costs associated with the creation of intangible assets are identified as belonging to either the **research** or **development** phase. Costs in the research phase are always expensed. Costs in the development phase are expensed unless the entity can demonstrate **all of the following**:

(1) Technical feasibility of completing the intangible asset;

(2) Intention to complete the intangible asset;

(3) Ability to use or sell it;

(4) Generation of future economic benefits – the existence of a market, or internal usefulness of the asset;

(5) Adequate resources (technical, financial, and other) to complete the development;

(6) Ability to measure reliably the expenditure attributable to the intangible asset during its development.

Costs include all expenditures directly attributed or allocable to creating, producing and preparing the asset from the date recognition criteria are met. Staff training costs, marketing costs and selling costs are excluded from development costs and expensed as incurred. Development costs initially expensed cannot be capitalized in a subsequent period. Normally, subsequent expenditures on an intangible asset after it has been acquired or completed must be expensed as incurred; under rare circumstances, asset recognition criteria may be met. It is important to note that **internally generated** goodwill, brands, mastheads, publishing titles, customer lists and items similar in substance **are not recognized as intangible assets**.

Subsequent Recognition

Intangible assets must be tested for impairment whenever changes in events or circumstances indicate an asset's carrying amount may not be recoverable. Goodwill and other assets with an indefinite life must be reviewed at least annually.

IAS 36 Impairment of Assets allows **reversals** of impairment losses under special circumstances, *except in the case of goodwill*.

The calculation of impairment calculation is performed at the Cash-Generating Unit (CGU) level for IFRS. The CGU is the *smallest identifiable group of assets that generates cash inflows that are largely independent of the cash inflows from other assets or groups of assets*. IFRS uses a one-step process. In this one-step process, an impairment loss is recognized if the asset's (or CGU's) carrying amount is greater than both its (discounted) fair value less cost to sell and its (discounted) value in use.

According to IFRS, an impairment loss identified at the CGU level is first applied against goodwill. Once goodwill has been eliminated, any remaining impairment is allocated to the other assets of the CGU on a prorated basis based on their carrying amounts.

An impairment identified in the current year is reported on the same line of the income statement as the amortization charge for the asset or, if it is material, in a separate line. The impairment loss is recorded against the revaluation surplus equity account to the extent that it reverses a previous revaluation for that asset.

Example 4-4 Intangible Assets: Initial Recognition and measurement

Muck AG has purchased an internet domain for which the following cost incurred:

Purchase price of the domain	285,000
Non-refundable VAT paid on the purchase of the trademark	2,850
Installation cost of IT/SocialMedia-Department	5,000
Research expenditures prior to the purchase of the domain	17,000
Legal fees in connection with the purchase	8,000
Salaries of personnel involved in the transaction	6,000

What is the measurement for the recognition of the domain as an intangible asset?

Intangible Assets are initially recognized *at cost*. The cost of a separately acquired intangible asset comprises the purchase price, including import duties and non-refundable purchase taxes after deducting trade discounts and rebates. Directly attributable cost of preparing the asset for its intended use are also included. The cost can usually be measured reliably, particularly when the purchase consideration is in the form of cash or other monetary assets.

In this case, the purchase price 285,000 + the non-refundable VAT 2,850 + the legal fees 8,000 = 295,850€ qualify as development cost and are an intangible asset.

4.4   Revenue from contracts with customers (IFRS 15)

As of 2018, IFRS 15 will replace the following standards and interpretations:

- IAS 18 Revenue,
- IAS 11 Construction Contracts
- SIC 31 Revenue – Barter Transaction Involving Advertising Services
- IFRIC 13 Customer Loyalty Programs
- IFRIC 15 Agreements for the Construction of Real Estate and
- IFRIC 18 Transfer of Assets from Customers

Contracts with customers will be presented in an entity's statement of financial position as a contract liability, a contract asset, or a receivable, depending on the relationship between the entity's performance and the customer's payment.

A contract liability is presented in the statement of financial position where a customer has paid an amount of consideration prior to the entity performing by transferring the related good or service to the customer.

Where the entity has performed by transferring a good or service to the customer and the customer has not yet paid the related consideration, a contract asset or a receivable is presented in the statement of financial position, depending on the nature of the entity's right to consideration. A contract asset is recognized when the entity's right to consideration is conditional on something other than the passage of time, for example future performance of the entity. A receivable is recognized when the entity's right to consideration is unconditional except for the passage of time.

Contract assets and receivables shall be accounted for in accordance with IFRS 9. Any impairment relating to contracts with customers should be measured, presented and disclosed in accordance with IFRS 9. Any difference between the initial recognition of a receivable and the corresponding amount of revenue recognized should also be presented as an expense, for example, an impairment loss.

So what is the difference between a "receivable" and a "contract asset"?

To start with, bear in mind that a contract asset is not the same as an account receivable. A contract asset is defined as "an entity's right to consideration in exchange for goods or services the entity has transferred to a customer that is *conditional* on something other than the passage of time (e.g., the performance of another obligation)."

If the right to this consideration is *unconditional* and only the passage of time is required before the consideration is due, then a receivable exists and a contract asset does not exist.

A customer's right to a refund does not make such consideration conditional because future refunds do not affect an entity's present right to obtain consideration. Such obligations should be treated as a separate refund liability.

Both receivables and contract assets are subject to credit risk; however, contract assets are also subject to other types of risks, such as performance risk – which means that the entity could find itself to be in a position not to be able to fulfill its obligation.

Impairment losses relating to a customer's credit risk (i.e., impairment of a contract asset or receivable) are measured based on the guidance in IFRS 9 Financial Instruments.

4.4.1   Five-Step Model Framework in IFRS 15

Every company must follow the five-step model in order to comply with IFRS 15. It will be sketched below.

Step 1: Identify the contract with the customer

IFRS 15 defines a contract as an agreement in which

- each party's rights in relation to the goods or services to be transferred can be identified;

- the payment terms for the goods or services to be transferred can be identified;

- the contract has commercial substance;

- and it is probable that the consideration to which the entity is entitled to in exchange for the goods or services will be collected.

Step 2: Identify the performance obligations in the contract

A performance obligation is a promise in a contract with a customer to transfer a good or a service to the customer.

Step 3: Determine the transaction price

The transaction price is the amount to which an entity expects to be entitled in exchange for the transfer of goods and services.

Where a contract contains elements of variable consideration, the entity will estimate the amount of variable consideration to which it will be entitled under the contract. Variable consideration can arise, for example, as a result of discounts, rebates, refunds, credits, price concessions, incentives, performance bonuses, penalties or other similar items. Variable consideration is also present if an entity's right to consideration is contingent on the occurrence of a future event.

Step 4: Allocate the transaction price to the performance obligations in the contracts

Where a contract has multiple performance obligations, an entity will allocate the transaction price to the performance obligations in the contract by reference to their relative standalone selling prices. If a standalone selling price is not directly observable, the entity will need to estimate it. IFRS 15 suggests various methods that might be used, including:

- Adjusted market assessment approach

- Expected cost plus a margin approach

- Residual approach (only permissible in limited circumstances).

Any overall discount compared to the aggregate of standalone selling prices is allocated between performance obligations on a relative standalone selling price basis. In certain circumstances, it may be appropriate to allocate such a discount to some but not all of the performance obligations.

Where consideration is paid in advance or in arrears, the entity will need to consider whether the contract includes a significant financing arrangement and, if so, adjust for the time value of money. A practical expedient is available where the interval between transfer of the promised goods or services and payment by the customer is expected to be less than 12 months.

Step 5: Recognize revenue when (or as) the entity satisfies a performance obligation

Revenue is recognized as control is passed, either over time or at a point in time.

Control of an asset is defined as the ability to direct the use of and obtain substantially all of the remaining benefits from the asset. This includes the ability to prevent others from directing the use of and obtaining the benefits from the asset. The benefits related to the asset are the potential cash flows that may be obtained directly or indirectly. These include, but are not limited to:

- using the asset to produce goods or provide services;

- using the asset to enhance the value of other assets;

- using the asset to settle liabilities or to reduce expenses;

- selling or exchanging the asset; pledging the asset to secure a loan; and holding the asset.

An entity recognizes revenue over time if one of the following criteria is met:

- the customer simultaneously receives and consumes all of the benefits provided by the entity as the entity performs;

- the entity's performance creates or enhances an asset that the customer controls as the asset is created;

  - or the entity's performance does not create an asset with an alternative use to the entity and the entity has an enforceable right to payment for performance completed to date.

If an entity does not satisfy its performance obligation over time, it satisfies it at a point in time. Revenue will therefore be recognized when control is passed at a certain point in time. Factors that may indicate the point in time at which control passes include, but are not limited to:

  - the entity has a present right to payment for the asset;

  - the customer has legal title to the asset;

  - the entity has transferred physical possession of the asset;

  - the customer has the significant risks and rewards related to the ownership of the asset;

  - and the customer has accepted the asset.

Example 4-5: Revenue Recognition in a telecommunications company

Muck Telecom AG entered into a contract with private customer Smith on July 1, 20X1 (t=0). Smith subscribes for Muck's monthly plan for 12 months, and in return, he receives a free phone from Muck. Smith will pay a monthly fee of 50€. Smith gets the phone right after signing the contract. Muck sells the same phones separately for 180€ and the same monthly plans for 40€ without the phone.

Step 1: Identify the contract with the customer

The contract is the obviously the written and signed contract between Muck and Smith.

Step 2: Identify the performance obligations in the contract

Two performance obligations, (1) Monthly plan for network services, (2) Phone device

Step 3: Determine the transaction price

The monthly fee: 50€

Months of subscription: 12 months

Total annual transaction price: $50 \times 12 = 600€$

Step 4: Allocate the transaction price to the performance obligations in the contracts

Performance obligation	Stand-alone selling price	Proportional	Allocated trans-action price	Revenue	Billing
Network	480	73%	0.73 × 600 = 438	438/12 = 36.50/month	50/month
Phone	180	27%	0.27 × 600 = 162	162	
Total	660	100%	600		

Step 5: Recognize revenue when (or as) the entity satisfies a performance obligation

Performance obligation	satisfied when?
Network services	over time, as monthly network services are provided
Phone	at one point in time, when delivered to customer

Journal entry for revenue of phone:

Debit record	Credit record
Contract asset 162€	Revenue from sale of goods 162€

Invoice for month 1 and customer payment:

Debit record	Credit record
Trade receivables 50€	Contract asset 13.5€
	Revenues from services 36.5€
Bank 50€	Trade receivables 50€

During the six months of 20X1, the company will present revenue from the phone device in the amount of 162 plus revenue from providing the network service in the amount of 219 (=6 × 36.5), in total 381. The contract asset will be carried at the end of 20X1 with 81 (= 162 − 6 × 13.5). In case the customer pays regularly, the payment will be credited towards the trade receivables.

What is the difference to the revenue recognition under IAS 18?

Under IAS 18 Muck Telecom AG would have applied the recognition criteria to the separately identifiable components of a single transaction (here: phone device + monthly plan). However, IAS 18 does not give any guidance on how to identify these components and how to allocate selling price and as a result, there were different practices applied.

For example, Muck could recognize the revenue from the sale of the monthly plan in full as the service is provided (revenue 50€ per month), and no revenue for the device – Muck could have treated the cost of the device as the cost of acquiring the customer.

For the simplicity, Muck would recognize no revenue from the sale of the device, because they give it away "for free". The cost of the device is recognized to profit or loss and effectively, Muck treats that as a cost of acquiring a new customer. IFRS 15 changes this, as the revenue is matched with the contractual obligations to be performed.

The difference in revenues for 20X1 is shown in the table:

Performance obligation	IAS 18	IFRS 15
Phone device	0	162
Network services	6 × 50 = 300	6 × 36.5 = 219
Total	*300*	*381*

4.4.2   Customer loyalty programs

Companies in the travel, hospitality and leisure industry often offer schemes to customers. These schemes usually comprise some option to purchase goods or services in the future by redeeming loyalty points. The company will need to consider whether the option the customer has represents a material right. Where this is the case, the customer is actually paying in advance for a future service. So the portion of the original transaction price must be allocated to that option and recognized as revenue when control of the goods or services associated with the option is transferred to the customer (e.g., when the loyalty points are redeemed or expire).

The following example has been taken from IASB's "Illustrative Example 52 IFRS 15 Revenue from Contracts with Customers" and commented for easier understanding.

Example 4-6: Customer Loyalty Program

An entity has a customer loyalty program that rewards a customer with one customer loyalty point for every €10 of purchases. Each point is redeemable for a €1 discount on any future purchases of the entity's products. During a reporting period, customers purchase products for €100,000 and earn 10,000 points that are redeemable for future purchases.

The consideration is fixed and the stand-alone selling price of the purchased products is €100,000. The entity expects 9,500 points to be redeemed. The entity estimates a stand-alone selling price of €0.95 per point (totaling €9,500) on the basis of the likelihood of redemption in accordance with IFRS 15.

The points provide a material right to customers that they would not receive without entering into a contract. Consequently, the entity concludes that the promise to provide points to the customer is a performance obligation.

Allocation of the transaction price

The entity allocates the transaction price (€100,000) to the product and the points on a relative stand-alone selling price basis as follows:

Product = 91,324 [€100,000 × (€100,000 stand-alone selling price ÷ €109,500)]

Points = 8,676 [€100,000 × (€9,500 stand-alone selling price ÷ €109,500)]

How to interpret these numbers?

As a matter of fact, the company had transactions of €100,000 (and has received €100,000), but for that price they gave away something that has a total value €109,500. Included in this transaction price is what the customers also bought and received – namely the right for future discounts. But this is just an obligation which has not yet been fulfilled by the company, so from the perspective of the company it is still a liability. But it is only a liability to the extent that the company expects these points to be redeemed. So the journal entries could look like

Debit record	Credit record
Cash/Bank €100,000	Revenue from sale of goods €91,324
	Contract liability €8,676

At the end of the first reporting period

Let us assume now that at the end of the first reporting period 4,500 points have been redeemed. Furthermore, the entity continues to expect 9,500 points to be redeemed in total.

The entity recognizes revenue for the loyalty points of €4,110 [(4,500 points ÷ 9,500 points) × €8,676] and recognizes a (remaining) contract liability of €4,566 (€8,676 – €4,110) for the unredeemed points at the end of the first reporting period.

The journal entry for this will be:

Debit record	Credit record
Contract liability €4,110	Revenue from loyalty points €4,110

At the end of the second reporting period

At the end of the second reporting period, 8,500 points have been redeemed cumulatively. The entity updates its estimate of the points that will be redeemed and now expects that 9,700 (instead of 9,500) points will be redeemed.

The entity recognizes revenue for the loyalty points of €3,493 {[(8,500 total points redeemed ÷ 9,700 total points expected to be redeemed) × €8,676 initial allocation] – €4,110 recognized in the first reporting period}. The journal entry for this will be:

Debit record	Credit record
Contract liability €3,493	Revenue from loyalty points €3,493

After that, the contract liability balance is €1,073 (€8,676 initial allocation – €7,603 of cumulative revenue recognized).

4.4.3 Revenue from Construction Projects

Under IAS 11, a construction contract is a contract specifically negotiated for the construction of an asset, (or combination of assets), that are closely interrelated or interdependent in terms of their design, technology and function or their ultimate purpose or use.

Construction projects will often not be finished within one accounting period. If that happens, additional accounting problems come up:

- How much of the project can be considered revenue of the period which should be included in profit or loss?
- If so, how much should be charged for related costs to that revenue?
- How much profit should be recognized in the period in respect of this contract?

With IFRS 15 though, many new concepts of revenue have been introduced for revenue and expense recognition. The most obvious change for construction contracts is that under IAS 11, recognition of revenue and profits on a percentage of completion basis was required where an arrangement met the the definition of a construction contract. Under IFRS 15, progressive revenue recognition will only be permitted where the enforceable contractual rights and obligations satisfy certain criteria. There is no automatic right to recognize revenue on a progressive basis for construction contracts. But when the criteria laid out in IFRS 15 are met, applying IFRS 15 to a traditional construction contract will result in an accounting outcome quite similar to the percentage-of-completion method.

From a general accounting point of view, three general revenue recognition models can be used:

Completed-Contract	*Percentage-of-Completion*	*Cost-Recovery*
Normally revenues and profits are only recognized in the income statement of once they are *realized*. However, the nature of construction contracts can mean that the contract is only invoiced and revenues realized on *completion of the contract*. This is the way German accounting (German Commercial Code) handles the recognition of revenue from construction contracts, and hence the method is called *Completed-Contract-Method*.	If the outcome can be measured reliably, revenue and costs on the contract should be measured so that contract revenue is matched with the contract costs incurred in reaching the stage of completion, resulting in the reporting of revenue, expenses and profit which can be attributed to the proportion of work completed.	If the outcome cannot be measured reliably, then no profit is recognized. Revenue is recognized only to the extent that costs are recoverable. Costs are recognized as an expense when incurred. Expected losses are required to be recognized as an expense as soon as a loss is probable.
Method according to German HGB (German Commercial Code)	Method according to IFRS	Method according to IFRS

From an accounting standpoint, **construction contracts** can come in two forms:

- A *fixed price contract* is a construction contract in which the contractor agrees to a fixed contract price, or a fixed rate per unit of output, which in some cases is subject to cost escalation clauses.
- A *cost plus contract* is a construction contract in which the contractor is reimbursed for allowable or otherwise defined costs, plus a percentage of these costs or a fixed fee.

Contract revenue

Comprises the initial amount agreed in the contract, plus revenue from variations in the original work, plus claims and incentive payments that:

- It is probable that they will result in revenue
- Can be measured reliably.

Revenue is to be measured at the fair value of the consideration received or receivable. In case of two or more contracts (same or different customers), these contracts should be accounted for as a single contract, if they have been negotiated together, the work is interrelated, and they are performed concurrently.

Estimation of outcome

Can be estimated reliably	Cannot be estimated reliably
Outcome can be reliably estimated if the entity can make an assessment of the revenue, the stage of completion and the costs to complete the contract.	No profit recognized
	Revenue recognized only to the extent costs are recoverable
If the outcome can be measured reliably - revenue and costs on the contract should be measured with reference to stage of completion basis. Under this basis, contract revenue is matched with the contract costs incurred in reaching the stage of completion, resulting in the reporting of revenue, expenses and profit which can be attributed to the proportion of work completed.	Costs are recognized as an expense when incurred
	Expected losses are required to be recognized as an expense as soon as a loss is probable.
When it is probable that the total contract costs will exceed contract revenue, the expected loss is recognized as an expense immediately.	

Difference between "work in progress" and "work in process"

In everyday language, the different terms might be treated as synonyms. And though there is no real norm about the terms, there are good arguments that from an accounting standpoint the two terms do *not* represent the same thing. We can differentiate between work in progress and work in process based on the *duration of the production cycle* and the category of assets being *current or non-current*.

- The term *work in process* is used for a manufacturer's inventory that is not yet completed. In an illustrative description these could be seen as the goods that are on the factory floor of a manufacturer and move from raw materials to finished product in a short period of time – indicating a *process*. The amount of work in process inventory would be reported along with Raw Materials Inventory and Finished Goods Inventory on the manufacturer's balance sheet as a *current asset*.

- The term *work in progress* is used the construction of long term assets (that will be used in the company's business) that are not yet completed. For example, if a company is constructing an addition to its building and the work is only partially completed, the amount spent so far would be recorded as work in progress or construction in progress, or construction work in progress (CWIP) and the account would be on the balance sheet as a long-term asset in the section entitled Property, Plant and Equipment. When the project is completed and put into service, the amount would be transferred out of CWIP and would be reported in the account Buildings within Property, Plant and Equipment.

- Companies producing items under a long-term (construction) contract often use an account entitled Construction in process or CIP – indicating that the item is not going to be a long-term asset used by the company itself, and also not a typical current asset (as it is being built over more than one period), but still some asset that is going to be sold to a customer.

Example 4-7: Basic Accounting Models for Construction Contracts

In 2013, Muck Bauprojekt AG contracted to build an office building for 3,000,000€. Construction was completed in 2015. Data relating to the contract are as follows:

in 1000€	2013	2014	2015
Costs incurred during the year	500	1,000	1,050
Estimated costs to complete as of year-end	2,000	1,000	0
Billings during the year	400	1,500	1,100
Cash collections during the year	350	1,050	1,600

Calculation of estimated gross profit in each year:

in 1000€	2013	2014	2015
Contract price	3,000	3,000	3,000
Actual costs to date	500	1,500	2,550
Estimated costs to complete	2,000	1,000	0
Total estimated costs	−2,500	−2,500	0
Estimated gross profit	500	500	
Total actual costs			−2,550
Actual gross profit			450

Completed contract method

Gross profit recognition

The idea here is very straightforward. The revenue will be recognized when it is realized. It is realized when the asset has been finished and delivered in 2015. After delivery, the contract price is earned, and the cost will be expensed. Until 2015, the work performed will be treated like unfinished inventory, as WIP (like work in progress) or CIP (construction in process).

in 1000€	2013	2014	2015
Gross profit	0	0	450

Journal entries

Year	Debit record	Credit record	Comment
2013	CIP 500 (BS)	Cash 500 (BS)	1
	Acc Receivable 400 (BS)	Contract work liability (BS) 400	2
	Cash 350 (BS)	Acc Receivable 350 (BS)	3
2014	CIP 1000 (BS)	Cash 1000 (BS)	1
	Acc Receivable 1500 (BS)	Contract work liability (BS) 1500	2
	Cash 1050 (BS)	Acc Receivable 1050 (BS)	3
2015	CIP 1050 (BS)	Cash 1050 (BS)	1
	Acc Receivable 1100 (BS)	Contract work liability (BS) 1100	2
	Cash 1600 (BS)	Acc Receivable 1600 (BS)	3
	Cost of Construction (IS) 2550 CIP (BS) 450	Revenue from long-term contracts (IS) 3000	
	Contract work liability (BS) 3000	CIP 3000	

1 various construction costs

2 Customer billed

3 Customer paid

Percentage-of-completion method (using cost-to-cost to estimate progress):

- For year 2013, 500 of 2,500 or 500/2,500 = 20 percent of total planned cost incurred. Hence, 20 percent of contract price will be recognized as revenue. The cost of 500 will be expense in the income statement, so the profit 2013 will be 600 – 500 = 100.

- For year 2014, an additional 1,000 in cost have incurred, so that accumulated cost is 1,500/2,500 = 60 percent of planned cost incurred. Hence, 60 percent of 3,000 = 1,800 should be recognized as revenues, of which 600 have been recognized in 2013 already. So for 2014, 1,200 will be recognized as revenue and 1,000 as construction costs. So the profit is 200.

- For the last year, the overall cost to date is 2,550 of 3,000 contract value, so the total gross profit is 450, of which 300 have been recorded in the 2013 and 2014 already:

in 1000€	2013	2014	2015
Cost incurred during the year	500	1,000	1,055
Recognized revenue	600	1,200	1,200
Gross profit of the year	100	200	150

Journal entries

Year	Debit record	Credit record
2013	CIP 500 (BS)	Cash 500 (BS)
	Acc Receivable 400 (BS)	Contract work liability (BS) 400
	Cash 350 (BS)	Acc Receivable 350 (BS)
	Cost of Construction 500 CIP 100	Revenue from l-t contract 600

Balance Sheet 2013			
CIP	600	Contr Liab	400
Acc Rec	50	Profit	100
Cash	-150		
	500		500

Year	Debit record	Credit record
2014	CIP 1000 (BS)	Cash 1000 (BS)
	Acc Receivable 1500 (BS)	Contract work liability (BS) 1500
	Cash 1050 (BS)	Acc Receivable 1050 (BS)
	Cost of Construction 1000 (PL) CIP 200 (BS)	Revenue from l-t contract 1200 (PL)

Balance Sheet 2014			
CIP	1800	Contr Liab	1900
Acc Rec	500	Profit	300
Cash	-100		
	2200		2200

Year	Debit record	Credit record
2015	CIP 1050 (BS)	Cash 1050 (BS)
	Acc Receivable 1100 (BS)	Contract work liability (BS) 1100
	Cash 1600 (BS)	Acc Receivable 1600 (BS)
	Cost of Construction (IS) 1050 CIP (BS) 150	Revenue from long-term contracts (IS) 3000
	Contract work liability (BS) 3000	WIP 3000

Balance Sheet 2015			
WIP	0	Contr Liab	0
Acc Rec	0	Profit	450
Cash	450		
	450		450

4.5   Leases (IAS 17, IFRS 16 as of 2019)

A lease is an agreement whereby the lessor conveys to the lessee the right to use an asset for an agreed period of time in return for a payment or series of payments.

IAS 17 differentiates between finance leases and operating leases:

- Finance lease: a lease that transfers substantially all the risks and rewards incidental to ownership of an asset. Title may or may not eventually be transferred.
- Operating lease: lease other than a finance lease.

The decisive question is whether a lease is *economically similar to purchasing the asset* being leased (the "underlying asset") or not. When a lease is determined to be economically similar to purchasing the underlying asset, the lease will be classified as a *finance lease* and reported on the company's balance sheet and an (artificial) liability will be calculated from the lease payments and also reported on the company's balance sheet.

There may be scenarios in which companies will prefer not to report additional liabilities in the balance sheet, because it may hurt financial metrics and eventually debt covenants – so they prefer operating leases to finance leases.

Leases not classified as finance leases are classified as operating leases and not reported on a company's balance sheet (they are what we call "off balance sheet leases"). *Off balance sheet leases* are accounted for similarly to *service contracts*, with the company reporting a *rental expense* in the income statement (typically the same amount in each period of the lease—a so called straight-line lease expense).

IFRS 16 – which will be effective as of 2019 – *eliminates the classification of leases as either operating leases or finance leases for a lessee*. Instead all leases are treated in a similar way to finance leases applying IAS 17 (exceptions apply for short-term leases of 12 months or less and for leases of low-value assets). Leases are then capitalized by recognizing the present value of the lease payments and showing them either as *lease assets ("right-of-use assets")* or together with property, plant and equipment. If lease payments are made over time, a company also recognizes a financial liability representing its obligation to make future lease payments.

For companies with material off balance sheet leases, IFRS 16 changes the nature of expenses related to those leases. IFRS 16 *replaces* the straight-line operating lease expense for those leases applying IAS 17 with a depreciation charge for the lease asset (included within operating costs) and an interest expense on the lease liability (included within finance costs). This change aligns the lease expense treatment for all leases. Although the depreciation charge is typically even, the interest expense reduces over the life of the lease as lease payments are made. This results in a reducing total expense as an individual lease matures.

The difference in the expense profile between IFRS 16 and IAS 17 is expected to be insignificant for many companies holding a portfolio of leases that start and end in different reporting periods.

Initial Recognition

Under IFRS a lease may be classified as either a **finance** or **operating lease**. The classification of finance lease occurs when substantially all the risks and rewards related to ownership are transferred from the lessor to the lessee. The classification of operating lease occurs when the risks and rewards related to ownership are not transferred from the lessor to the lessee.

IFRS uses five lease criteria that are **indicators** of a finance lease. The five criteria include:

(1) The lessee acquires ownership of the leased asset at the conclusion of the lease.

(2) The lessee has a bargain purchase option.

(3) The term of the lease covers the majority of the leased asset's economic life.

(4) The present value of minimum lease payments is equivalent to nearly all of the leased asset's fair value.

(5) Leased assets are of a specialized nature and are only usable by the lessee unless substantial adjustments are made to the asset.

IFRS also provides three criteria that could lead to a finance lease including:

(6) Upon early termination of the lease, the lessee is responsible for the lessor's losses

(7) Any gains and losses due to the fluctuation in the fair value of the residual are attributed to the lessee

(8) The lessee has the option to continue the lease for a secondary period for a below market rate.

Meeting only one of the eight criteria leads to financial lease classification.

IFRS does not provide specific percentages for determining the majority of the leased asset's economic life or substantially all of the leased asset's fair value and therefore requires some professional judgment.

Table 4-2: Lessor and Lessee Accounting

Lessor Accounting	Lessee Accounting
Operating Leasing. IAS 17 requires the leased asset meeting the criteria of an operating lease to be recognized by the lessor on the balance sheet and depreciated over its economic life in a manner consistent with IAS 16 and IAS 38. Income resulting from the leased asset should be recognized on the income statement on a straight line basis or in a manner that more appropriately represents the transfer of benefits.	**Operating Leases.** Payments made by the lessee should be recognized as expense either on a straight line basis over the lease term or in a manner that more appropriately represents the transfer of benefits.
Finance Leases. IFRS specifies that leased assets meeting the finance lease criteria should be recorded in the balance sheet as a receivable equal to the net investment in the lease. According to IFRS, minimum lease payments for a lessor include guarantees from the lessee, related party of the lessee, or third party that is not related to the lessor. Income from the lease is recognized at a constant periodic rate of return, receipt of capital and finance income, attributable to the lessor's net investment in the finance lease.	**Finance Leases.** The lessee should recognize the leased asset as both an asset and liability on the balance sheet at the lower of fair value or the present value of minimum lease payments. IFRS normally uses the *interest rate implicit in the lease* to calculate the present value of the minimum lease payments. The lessee's *incremental borrowing rate* may be used if the implicit rate is unknown. Depreciation on the finance lease should be calculated according to *IAS 16 Property, Plant and Equipment* and *IAS 38 Intangible Assets*.

Sale and Leaseback Transactions

According to IFRS, the type of lease determines the accounting treatment of a sale and leaseback transaction. Profit from a finance sale and leaseback transaction is **deferred and amortized**. Accounting for profit from an operating sale and leaseback transaction depends on whether the transaction is at fair value. A sale at fair value requires immediate recognition. A sale at below fair value requires immediate recognition unless the lower value is made up for by lower future rentals. A sale above fair value requires the amount above fair value to be deferred over the period the asset will be used.

Example 4-8 Lease Contract

Muck Company, as lessee, enters into a lease agreement on July 1, 2008, for equipment. The following data are relevant to the lease agreement:

1. The term of the non-cancelable lease is 4 years, with no renewal option. Payments of 395,000€ are due on June 30 of each year.
2. The cost of the equipment on July 1, 2008 is 1,400,000€. The equipment has an economic life of 6 years with no salvage value.
3. Muck depreciates similar machinery it owns on a straight-line basis.

4. The lessee pays all executory costs.

5. Muck's incremental borrowing rate is 10% per year. The lessee is aware that the lessor used an implicit rate of 8% in computing the lease payments (present value factor for 4 periods at 8%, 3.31212684; at 10%, 3.169865446).

Which type of lease has Muck Company entered into? Which accounting treatment is applicable? What is the annual straight-line depreciation expense? What is the interest expense portion (in case of a finance lease) and the calculated payback amounts included in the leasing fee?

Step 1: Determine the present value of the leasing fees

IFRS normally uses the interest rate implicit in the lease to calculate the present value of the minimum lease payments. The lessee's incremental borrowing rate may be used if the implicit rate is unknown. Since we know the lessor used an implicit rate of 8 percent, we determine the Present Value of an Annuity Factor (PVAF) with i=0.08 and n=4:

$$PVAF(i=0.08; n=4) = \frac{(1+i)^n - 1}{(1+i)^n \times i} = \frac{(1.08)^4 - 1}{(1.08)^4 \times 0.08} = 3.31212684$$

The present value of leasing fees is therefore 395,000€ × 3.31212684 = **1,308,290€**.

Step 2: Apply the lease criteria IAS 17

Critera No.	IAS Leasing Criteria	Evaluation
1	Transfer of ownership-Test	no contract provision
2	Bargain Purchase Option-Test	no contract provision
3	Economic-Life-Test (major part of the economic life?)	4/6 = 67%. So no.
4	Recovery-of-Investment-Test (PV of leasing fees > 90 % asset cost?)	=1308290/1400000 = 93,4% **YES**
5	Special Lease-Test	no

There is evidence that the leasing fees that Muck pays cover almost all the total cost for the asset. This is a strong indication that Muck can be regarded as the economic owner of the asset. The contract would probably we classified as a finance lease. In case of a finance lease, the lessee will recognize the leased asset *as both an asset and liability* on the balance sheet at the *lower of fair value or the present value of minimum lease payments*. The lessee will recognize the asset as if he had purchased it on credit, so he will also recognize depreciation expense for the asset.

Muck will recognize the leased asset on the statement of financial position at the present value of lease payments (all amounts have been rounded to full € for ease of reading) and treat the contract as a purchase financed by a loan.

Year	carrying value (1)	depreciation (2)	liability (3)	allocation of leasing fee		
				interest (4)	payback (5)	leasing fee (6)
01.07.08	1.308.290		1.308.290			
30.06.09	981.218	327.073	1.017.953	104.663	290.337	395.000
30.06.10	654.145	327.073	704.389	81.436	313.564	395.000
30.06.11	327.073	327.073	365.741	56.351	338.649	395.000
30.06.12	0	327.073	0	29.259	365.741	395.000
		1.308.290		**271.710**	**1.308.290**	**1.580.000**

Column	Explanation
1	Asset value in the balance sheet, net of depreciation
2	Straight-line depreciation, allocation of cost over useful life, expense in IS
3	Carrying value of liability, after reduction by amount in (5)
4	part of the leasing fee recognized as an expense in the IS
5	part of leasing fee attributed as a payback of liability
6	The leasing fee is divided into interest expense and reduction of liability

4.6   Inventories (IAS 2)

According to IFRS, inventories are assets:

- Held for sale in the ordinary course of business;
- Being produced for sale in the ordinary course of business;
- In the form of materials or supplies to be used in production or to provide services.

Initial Recognition

IFRS measures inventories *initially at cost*. Inventories are classified as current assets on the face of the balance sheet, because they *are expected to be realized within the entity's normal operating cycle*. The standard requires entities to disclose the composition of inventory in the financial statements.

Which costs are included?

To determine cost, the standard includes the costs of purchase, costs of conversion, and costs to bring the inventories to their current location and condition. According to *IAS 2 Inventories*, costs to bring the inventories to their current condition could include specific design expenses. Selling costs, general administrative costs, and most storage costs from the cost of inventory are not included, as they are not considered inventoriable cost.

Which costs are not included?

IAS 2 says: Inventory cost should not include

- abnormal waste
- storage costs
- administrative overheads unrelated to production
- selling costs foreign
- exchange differences arising directly on the recent acquisition of inventories invoiced in a foreign currency
- interest cost when inventories are purchased with deferred settlement terms.

What is this with the "abnormal waste" and other items not to include?

The costs of conversion of inventories include costs directly related to the units of production, such as direct labor – but not material cost. They also include a systematic allocation of fixed and variable production overheads that are incurred in converting materials into finished goods. Fixed production overheads are those indirect costs of production that remain relatively constant regardless of the volume of production, such as depreciation and maintenance of factory buildings and the cost of factory management and administration. Variable production overheads are those indirect costs of production that vary directly, or nearly directly, with the volume of production, such as indirect materials.

The allocation of fixed production overheads for the purpose of their inclusion in the costs of conversion is based on the *normal capacity of the production facilities*. Normal capacity is the production expected to be achieved on an average over a number of periods or seasons under normal circumstances, taking into account the loss of capacity resulting from planned maintenance.

The actual level of production may be used if it approximates normal capacity. The amount of fixed production overheads allocated to each unit of production is not increased as a consequence of low production or idle plant. Unallocated overheads are recognized as an expense in the period in which they are incurred. In periods of abnormally high production, the amount of fixed production overheads allocated to each unit of production is decreased so that inventories are not measured above cost. Variable production overheads are assigned to each unit of production on the basis of the actual use of the production facilities.

Keep in mind that the more cost are included in the inventory values the less are recognized as expenses in PL. If the company includes excessive waste or other fixed cost above normal capacity, they would keep these cost out of PL (increasing profit) whereas the actual performance is just the opposite – incurring higher cost than normal. In that case, because of the capitalization of cost in the inventories, the company would appear wealthier than it really is. Apart from that, there would be a dysfunctional incentive on management to incur higher overheads and waste.

Example 4-9: Inventories and abnormal waste

Business hasn't gone well in the last year for Muck AG. On January 1, 2013, Muck AG signed a special order contract to manufacture custom-design generators for a new customer. The customer requests that the generators be ready for pickup by June 15, 2013 and guarantees it will take possession of the generators by July 15, 2013. Muck incurred the following direct costs related to the custom-designed generators:

Cost item	in €
Cost to complete the design of the generators	3,000
Purchase price for materials and parts	80,000
Transportation cost to get materials and parts to manufacturing facility	2,000
Direct labor (10,000 labor hours at €12 per hour)	120,000
Cost to store finished product (from June 15 to June 30)	2,000

Because of Muck AG's inexperience in manufacturing generators of this design, the cost of materials and parts included an abnormal amount of waste totaling €5,000. In addition to direct costs, Muck applied variable and fixed overhead to inventory using predetermined rates. The variable overhead rate is €2 per direct labor hour. The fixed overhead rate based on a normal level of production is €6 per direct labor hour. Given the decreased level of production expected in 2013, Muck estimates a fixed overhead application rate of €9 per direct labor hour in 2013.

The inventory should be measured as follows (values in €):

Cost item	in €
Cost to complete the design of the generators	3,000
Purchase price for materials and parts	80,000
./. abnormal waste	- 5,000
Transportation cost to get materials and parts to manufacturing facility	2,000
Direct labor (10,000 labor hours at €12 per hour)	120,000
Variable overhead (10,000 labor hours at €2 per hour)	20,000
Fixed overhead (10,000 labor hours at €6 per hour based on normal level of production)	60,000
Cost of inventory	*280,000*

The fixed overhead application rate based on a normal level of production is used per IAS 2.13. The actual level of production can be used if it approximates the normal level; however, the actual level of production in 2013 does not approximate the normal level. Storage costs are excluded from the cost of inventory per IAS 2.16, which indicates that storage costs are excluded from the cost of inventories unless they are necessary in the production process before a further production stage.

Example 4-10: Inventories and operating at below normal capacity

Where an entity operates at normal capacity, overhead costs would normally be included in inventory and later recognized as cost of sales when the product is sold. The requirement of IAS 2 effectively accelerates the recognition of these costs in the income statement.

Muck AG has been operating at below normal capacity. The following data apply.

Fixed production overhead items	in €
Factory manager's wage	1,500
Other fixed production overheads	1,500
Variable production overhead costs 2.50/unit, made up from - Indirect labour 1,125 - Indirect materials, supplies 750	1,875
Total fixed production overheads	3,000

So the overhead recovery rate is calculated as

Fixed production overhead / Direct costs = 3,000/7,500 = 40%

The overhead recovery rate indicates the rate at which overhead is recovered in relation to direct production cost. In this example, the overhead recovery rate is 40 percent, implying that for each Euro of direct production cost incurred, an additional €0.40 of production overhead are incurred and recovered when operating at below normal capacity. However, IAS 2.13 states that the amount of overhead allocated to each unit of production is not increased as a consequence of low production or idle plant. Muck AG therefore would revert to the overhead recovered when operating at normal capacity, being 30 percent, by adjusting the calculation of actual capacity utilized (i.e. 75%).

Producing at normal capacity, the following data would apply:

Normal capacity data	units
Normal capacity	1,000
Theoretical capacity	1,200
Actual capacity utilized (75 percent of normal capacity)	750
Total fixed production overheads	3,000

In this example, normal capacity is 83% of theoretical capacity. In practice, normal capacity is the true "full" capacity level – the theoretical level is ignored when allocating fixed production overheads. The typical plant is designed under specific conditions which technologically enable it to produce at a theoretical production level or capacity. In practice, however, the actual plant capabilities envisage a normal production capacity, which effectively represents the full or maximum capacity and is generally below the theoretical capacity level.

Production overhead recognized as part of cost of inventory is:

Direct costs × overhead recovery rate × actual capacity utilization rate =

$7,500 \times 40\% \times 75\% = 2,250$

Therefore, the fixed overhead cost per unit is:

Fixed production overhead recognized as inventory / actual units produced =

$2,250/750 = 3.0$

As indicated above, the amount of fixed overhead allocated to each unit of production is not increased as a consequence of low production or idle plant [IAS 2.13]. Consequently, the cost per unit is 3.0, which is the same as it is when operating at normal capacity. Muck would have arrived at the same cost allocation had he simply applied the normal recovery rate of 30 percent to direct costs incurred (i.e. $7,500 \times 30\% = 2,250$). Variable production overheads are fully allocated to the cost of inventory (i.e. $1,875/750 = 2.50/unit$).

In the determination of production overhead recognized as part of the cost of inventory, the production capacity is taken into account. In this case normal capacity is below (theoretically) full capacity. At normal capacity, conceptually, fixed production overhead is considered to be 100% efficient and is presumed to be fully employed in the production process, and is therefore fully recognized as part of the cost of inventory.

However, once below normal capacity, production overhead costs are discounted for any shortfall and not considered to be fully engaged in the production process and therefore are not fully recognized as part of inventory cost.

Therefore, fixed production overhead recognized as an expense is:

Total production overhead – production overhead allocated to inventory =

3,000 – 2,250 = 750.

The remaining 750 is recognized as an expense in the income statement, as part of cost of sales. The 750 represents the portion of production overhead costs unallocated to inventories, as they are presumed to not contribute to the production process as a result of production being below normal capacity, whilst the fixed overhead cost is incurred – irrespective of the volume of production.

In this case, the actual production is 25% below full capacity, which translates to a cost of 750 (i.e., 3,000 × 25% = 750). If production was at 100% of normal capacity, the full amount of production overheads would be allocated to inventory. Therefore, the 750 essentially represents the portion of fixed production overheads not employed in the production process (cost of idle capacity) when operating at below normal capacity and therefore not contributing to bringing inventory to its present location and condition.

Cost flow assumptions

IAS 2 allows entities to use the **FIFO** or **weighted average methods**. The FIFO method follows the assumption that items purchased or produced first are sold first and the ending inventory is made up of items recently purchased or produced. The weighted average method prices inventory based on the average cost of similar items purchased or produced throughout the period. IAS 2 prohibits entities from using the last in, last out (LIFO) method of inventory valuation. The LIFO method assumes that items purchased or produced last are sold first and the ending inventory is made up of items purchased or produced first.

Changing the cost flow assumption may have a significant impact on the *carrying value* of inventory and on profit. Learners should make sure they understand the effect that increasing or decreasing purchase prices for materials or merchandise have under the two different cost flow assumptions LIFO and FIFO

Table 4-3: Cost flow assumption and effect on profit with changes in purchase prices

Cost flow assumption	Material use or merchandise consumption valued with prices from	Inventory at BS date measured with prices from	If purchase prices *increase* during the period, then...	If purchase prices *decrease* during the period, then...
LIFO	later in the period (new prices)	early in the period (old prices)	...profit is **lower**, because (1) material or merchandise expenses are measured with new = higher prices and (2) inventory is measured at lower prices from early in the period.	...profit is **higher**, because (1) material or merchandise expenses are measured with new = lower prices and (2) inventory is measured at higher prices from early in the period.
FIFO	early in the period (old prices)	later in the period (new prices)	...profit is **higher**, because (1) material or merchandise expenses are measured with new = lower prices and (2) inventory is measured at higher prices from early in the period.	...profit is **lower**, because (1) material or merchandise expenses are measured with new = higher prices and (2) inventory is measured at lower prices from early in the period.

Subsequent Recognition

According to IFRS, inventory should be written down *if it declines in value below its original cost*. IAS 2 Inventories requires inventories to be measured *at the lower of cost and net realizable value*. Net realizable value is defined by IAS 2 as *"the estimated selling price in the ordinary course of business less the estimated costs of completion and the estimated costs necessary to make the sale."* According to IFRS, the journal entry to write down inventory debits Inventory write down expense and credits inventory. IAS 2 requires entities to reverse the value of inventory previously written down when there is a subsequent increase in the inventory's value. Reversals are limited to the amount of the original write down.

To write down inventory, entities can use the *direct or indirect method*. The journal entry under the direct method debits cost of goods sold and credits inventory. The journal entry under the indirect method debits loss due to market decline of inventory and credits allowance to reduce inventory to market.

4.7   Financial Instruments

IFRS 9 is effective for annual periods beginning on or after January 1, 2018. IFRS 9 super-sedes IAS 39, Financial Instruments: Recognition and Measurement. IAS 39 was created with pre-defined asset class categories like

- Trading assets/liabilites,
- Available for sale,
- Held to maturity and
- Loans/Receivables.

The loans and receivables assets (and HTM) under IAS 39 were valued on the basis of amortized cost. Other categories use fair value. From an accounting perspective, variations in valuation are posted to OCI for AFS assets; otherwise all variations are posted to profit and loss (P&L).

4.7.1   Financial Instruments according to IAS 39

There are four basic categories of financial assets according to IAS 39 (Table 4-4).

Table 4-4 Main categories financial assets IAS 39

Financial asset at fair value through profit or loss	A financial asset that is either - classified as held for trading, or - upon initial recognition it is designated by the entity as at fair value through profit or loss.
Held-to-maturity financial investments	Non-derivative financial assets with fixed or determinable payments and fixed maturity that an entity has the positive intention to hold to maturity, other than: - those designated at fair value through profit or loss upon initial recognition; - those designated as available for sale and; - those that meet the definition of loans and receivables.
Loans and receivables	- Non-derivative financial assets that are created by the enterprise by providing money, goods or services directly to a debtor, other than those that are originated with the intent to be sold immediately or in the short term, which should be classified as held-for-trading [available for sale]. - Examples of items in the loans and receivables category include accounts receivable and loans to other entities.
Available-for-sale financial assets	Non-derivative financial assets designated as available for sale or are not classified in any other of 3 above categories.

Table 4-5 Main categories financial liabilities IAS 39

Financial liabilities at fair value through profit or loss	A financial liability that is either - classified as held for trading, or - upon initial recognition it is designated by the entity as at fair value through profit or loss
Other financial liabilities	measured at amortized cost using the effective interest method

However, no matter how the financial instrument would be initially classified, IAS 39 permits entities to initially **designate** the instrument at fair value through profit or loss (but fair value must be reliably measured). In plain language, it means the company can just determine this as it sees fit. Initial classification of financial assets and financial liabilities is critical due to their subsequent measurement.

Embedded derivatives

An embedded derivative is a component of a hybrid instrument that also includes a non-derivative host contract.

A typical example is a rental contract concluded for several years in advance with rental price adjustments according to inflation measured by the consumer price index in the European Union. The non-derivative part in this case is a rent of some property or facility. An embedded derivative part is then forward contract indexed to the consumer price index in EU.

IAS 39 requires separation of an embedded derivative from the host contract when the following conditions are fulfilled:

- the economic risks and characteristics of the embedded derivative are not closely related to the economic risks and characteristics of the host contract. This may be the case when the rent of property is somehow dependent on changes in EU consumer price index;
- a separate instrument with the same terms as the embedded derivative would meet the definition of a derivative;
- the hybrid instrument (whole rental contract in our example) is not measured at fair value with changes in fair value recognized in the income statement.

Separation means to account for an embedded derivative separately in line with *IAS 39* and the host contract (the rent in this case) in line with another appropriate standard. If an entity is not able to do this, then the whole contract must be accounted for as a financial asset at fair value through profit or loss.

Initial recognition and measurement

IAS 39 requires recognizing a financial asset or a financial liability in the balance sheet when the entity becomes a party to the contractual provisions of the instrument.

Derivatives shall also be recognized in the statement of financial position (balance sheet). Note that the fair value of derivatives may change significantly having an impact on the profit or loss and the statement of financial position.

Financial asset or financial liability shall be initially measured at its fair value. When financial asset or financial liability are **not** measured at fair value through profit or loss, then directly attributable transaction costs shall be included in the initial measurement.

Subsequent Measurement

Valuation changes subsequent to the initial purchase are accounted for under IFRS are depicts in the following table.

Table 4-6 Subsequent measurement financial instruments

Category	Measurement	Statement
Financial assets		
Financial assets at fair value through profit or loss (FVTPL)	Fair value	Profit or loss (IS)
Held-to-maturity financial investments	Amortized cost using the effective interest method	Profit or loss (IS)
Loans and receivables		Profit or loss (IS)
Available-for-sale financial investments except below	Fair value	Other comprehensive income (except for impairment and foreign exchange gain/loss)
Investments in equity instruments with no reliable fair value measurement and derivatives linked to them	Cost	Impairment to profit or loss
Financial assets designated as hedged items	(Hedge Accounting)	(Hedge Accounting)
Derivative financial assets	Fair value	Profit or loss (IS)
Financial liabilities		
Financial liabilities at fair value through profit or loss	Fair value	Profit or loss (IS)
Other financial liabilities	Amortized cost using the effective interest method	Profit or loss (IS)
Financial liabilities designated as hedged items	(Hedge Accounting)	(Hedge Accounting)
Derivative financial liabilities	Fair value	Profit or loss
Financial liabilities arising when transfer of financial asset does not qualify for derecognition or is accounted using continuing-involvement method	Measured in line with specific IAS 39 provisions related to transfers / continuing involvement	Profit or loss

Table 4-7 Decision path Financial Instruments IAS 39

- Derivatives other than for hedging? - Financial asset held for trading? - Designated to the FVTPL category?			
yes	*no*		
	- Possible default risk (not credit risk)? - No determinable payments? - Designated to the Available-for-sale (AFS) category?		
	yes	*no*	
		Quoted on an active market?	
		yes	*no*
		Fixed maturity and entity has positive intent and ability to hold to maturity?	
		no | *yes*	
Category: *at fair value through profit or loss*	*Category:* *Available-for-sale* (AFS)	*Category:* *Held-to-maturity*	*Category:* *Loans and Receivables*
Measured at: Fair value with all gains and losses being recognized in profit or loss.	*Measured at:* - Fair value with gains and losses recognized in other comprehensive income - Impairment losses and foreign exchange differences are recognized in profit or loss.	*Measured at:* Amortized cost using the effective interest method, less impairment losses.	

Impairment

An entity shall assess at the end of each reporting period whether there is any objective evidence that a financial asset is impaired. If there is such evidence, then an entity must calculate the amount of impairment loss.

Impairment loss is calculated as a *difference between the asset's carrying amount and the present value of estimated cash flows discounted at the financial asset's original effective interest rate*. Impairment loss shall be recognized to profit or loss account.

Reversal of the impairment loss is possible, but only if in a subsequent period the impairment loss decreases and the decrease directly relates to some event occurring after the recognition of impairment loss. Reversal shall be re recognized in profit or loss.

Equity Instruments

IFRS determines the method of accounting for equity instruments *based on the level of control the investor has over the organization.*

- Holdings for which the investor *lacks significant influence* are accounted for using the *fair value method.* IFRS presumes an investor lacks significant influence over a company if he holds less than 20 percent of the voting power, unless there is evidence to the contrary. For investments in unlisted equity instruments, IFRS requires the instrument to be measured at fair value if it can be determined, otherwise at cost.

- IFRS accounts for investments in which the investor has *significant influence* over the company using the equity method. *Significant influence* is assumed when the investor is holding between 20 percent and 50 percent of the voting power – but owning less than 50 percent is considered a lack of control over the company. The asset position is called *investment in associate.* According to *IAS 28 Investment in Associates,* the initial recognition of the investment is at cost and the investor's share of profit or loss increases or decreases the carrying amount of the investment. Distributions decrease the carrying amount and changes in the investor's share of the associate's reserves increase or decrease the carrying amount. *IAS 28* classifies *investments in associates* accounted for using the *equity method* as noncurrent assets and requires separate line disclosure on the balance sheet. The investor's share of profit or loss must be reported on the income statement.

According to IFRS, the parent and subsidiary must use uniform accounting policies in the consolidated financial statements – but it allows the parent and subsidiary to have different reporting dates as long as there is not more than a three month difference.

4.7.2   Financial Instruments according to IFRS 9 (as of 2018)

IFRS 9 will replace IAS 39 completely. As the IASB completes each phase, it will delete the relevant portions of IAS 39 and create replacement chapters in IFRS 9. Its effective date is 1 January 2018.

IFRS 9 applies a classification and measurement model for financial assets, dependent on both:

- The entity's business model objective for managing financial assets
- The contractual cash flow characteristics of financial assets.

IFRS 9 presupposes that there are two general motivations to hold financial assets:

(1) An entity can buy a financial asset that it plans to sell at a profit. To do so, there must be a future buyer and probably a market of buyers. Such financial instruments will normally be valued at fair value, if the business model reflects this type of

transaction. Most of its profit comes from the resale, though some income may accrue from interest, or dividends, while it is held.

(2) An entity can provide a loan to another party, hold it to maturity, and collect the interest and principal repayments. Its profit is derived from the client. It will normally be measured at amortized cost, but only if the business model reflects this type of transaction.

An entity will designate a financial asset as measured at fair value through profit or loss ('FVTPL'), if this reflects the business model. An entity may have more than one business model (different portfolios of financial instruments).

Also, it uses FVTPL if it eliminates, or significantly reduces, a measurement or recognition inconsistency (an 'accounting mismatch'), that would otherwise arise from measuring assets or liabilities, or recording the gains and losses on them, on different bases.

Recognition and measurement

A financial instrument is initially recognized when the entity becomes a party to the contractual provisions of the instrument.

Subsequent classification and measurement

IFRS 9 specifies how an entity should classify and measure financial assets, including some hybrid contracts. They require all financial assets to be

a. classified on the basis of the entity's business model for managing the financial assets and the contractual cash flow characteristics of the financial asset;

b. initially measured at fair value plus particular transaction costs, except in the case of a financial asset at fair value through profit or loss, when the transaction costs are expensed;

c. subsequently measured at fair value, or amortized cost.

The accounting for financial liabilities is unchanged from IAS 39, except that credit-value adjustments are generally recorded through OCI.

Table 4-8 Decision path Financial Instruments IFRS 9

Is the objective of the entity's business model to hold the financial assets to collect contractual cash flows?			
Yes			No
Is the financial asset held to achieve an objective by both collecting contractual cash flows and selling financial assets?			
Yes		No	
Do contractual cash flows represent solely payments of principal and interest?			
Yes	No		
Amortized cost	FVTOCI (no recycling)	FVTPL	

Example 4-11: Fixed-income security at amortized cost – effective interest rate method

At the beginning of 2010, Muck AG buys a 5-year security (e.g. a bond) with par value of €100,000 to be repaid at maturity. The security pays 6 percent interest (on par value) at the end of each year. The risk-adjusted yield-to-maturity for this security is 7.64 percent (rounded), so the security is purchased with a discount of 6,600€.

The amortized cost at each year represent the present value of the loan discounted with the YTM.

Year	Amortized Cost at beginning of year (a)	Interest income end of year (b=a × 0.0764...)	Cash flow at end of year (c)	Amortized Cost at end of year (d=a+b-c)	Deferred interest income (e=b-c)
2010	93,400	7,133	6,000	94,533	1,133
2011	94,533	7,220	6,000	95,753	1,220
2012	95,753	7,313	6,000	97,066	1,313
2013	97,066	7,413	6,000	98,479	1,413
2014	98,479	7,521	6,000	100,000	1,521

The actual interest income is based on the YTM and it is accrued over the lifetime of the security. The journal entries for years 2010 to 2014 are as follows:

2010 (beginning)

Debit record	Credit record
Financial asset 100,000€	Cash 93,400€ Deferred interest income 6,600€

2010 (end)

Debit record	Credit record
Cash 6,000€ Deferred interest income 1,133	Interest income 7,133€

2011 (end)

Debit record	Credit record
Cash 6,000€ Deferred interest income 1,220	Interest income 7,220€

2012 (end)

Debit record	Credit record
Cash 6,000€ Deferred interest income 1,313	Interest income 7,313€

2013 (end)

Debit record	Credit record
Cash 6,000€ Deferred interest income 1,413	Interest income 7,413€

2014 (end)

Debit record	Credit record
Cash 106,000€ Deferred interest income 1,521	Interest income 7,521€ Financial asset 100,000€

4.8   Depreciation and Impairment

4.8.1   Depreciation

According to IFRS, entities are required to depreciate PPE on a systematic basis. IFRS does not require entities to use a particular method of depreciation. According to IAS 16 Property, Plant and Equipment, the method of depreciation should reflect *the expected pattern of consumption of the future economic benefits embodied in the asset.*

It is also required to depreciate items of PPE that are idle, but not to depreciate items of *PPE held for sale*. IFRS requires the estimates of useful life, residual value, and the method of depreciation to be reviewed on an annual basis. Depreciation method, residual value, and useful life may occur and are treated as a change in accounting estimate.

Component depreciation specifies that any part or portion of PPE that can be *separately identified as an asset* should be depreciated over its useful life. IFRS requires component depreciation if components of an asset *have differing patterns of benefits*. If components of an asset have different useful lives, the entity should identify the components and separately account for them.

4.8.2   Impairment of assets IAS 36

According to IFRS, a company must record a write-off when the carrying amount of an asset is not *recoverable*. Under *IAS 36 Impairment of Assets*, an asset is impaired when its recoverable amount is less than its carrying amount.

- The *recoverable amount* is the greater of net selling price and value in use.
- *Net selling price* is the market value of the asset less disposal costs.
- *Value in use* is the present value of future net cash flows expected over the remaining life of the asset.
- The impairment loss is the difference between the asset's carrying value and its recoverable amount and it is recognized in income.

For assets using the revaluation model, impairment is usually only recognized if disposal costs are significant, causing the recoverable amount (fair value less disposal costs) to be less than the carrying amount (fair value). When an asset is carried at a revalued amount, the impairment loss is taken against the revaluation surplus and any remainder is taken against income. According to IFRS, write-ups for subsequent recoveries of impairment are permitted. For the cost model, the write-up of the asset cannot exceed what the carrying value would have been if no impairment loss had been recognized.

4.8.3   Impairment of receivables

Receivables in IAS 39

According to IFRS, *loans and receivables* was one of four financial assets categories. *IAS 39 Financial Instruments: Recognition and Measurement* defines loans and receivables as "financial assets that are created by the enterprise by providing money, goods or services directly to a debtor". The category of loans and receivables *does not include the following*:

- Loans and receivables that an entity has designated as *held at fair value with gains or loss going through profit or loss*;
- Loans and receivables classified as *held for trading* because an entity intends to sell them in the near future;

- Loans and receivables designated as *available for sale*;

- Loans and receivables that the holder may not recover substantially all of its initial investment.

Examples of items in the loans and receivables category include accounts receivable and loans to other entities. IAS 39 required loans and receivables to be measured initially at fair value. Valuation changes subsequent to the initial purchase are accounted for *at amortized cost using the effective interest method*. IFRS requires financial assets including loans and receivables to be reported on the face of the balance sheet. Loans and receivables are classified as current if they are *expected to be realized within 12 months or the normal operating cycle*. Otherwise, the loans and receivables are classified as non-current.

Entities following IFRS may sub-classify receivables as receivables from trade customers and receivables from related parties and other amounts.

The general impairment approach in IFRS 9

In 2014, the IASB issued the final version of IFRS 9 incorporating a new expected loss impairment model and introducing limited amendments to the classification and measurement requirements for financial assets.

IFRS 9's general approach to recognizing impairment is based on a three-stage process which is intended to reflect the deterioration in credit quality of a financial instrument.

- Stage 1 covers instruments that have not deteriorated significantly in credit quality since initial recognition or (where the optional low credit risk simplification is applied) that have low credit risk.

- Stage 2 covers financial instruments that have deteriorated significantly in credit quality since initial recognition (unless the low credit risk simplification has been applied and is relevant) but that do not have objective evidence of a credit loss event.

- Stage 3 covers financial assets that have objective evidence of impairment at the reporting date. 12-month expected credit losses are recognized in stage 1, while lifetime expected credit losses are recognized in stages 2 and 3.

IFRS 9 draws a distinction between financial instruments that have not deteriorated significantly in credit quality since initial recognition and those that have:

- '12-month expected credit losses' are recognized for the first of these two categories. 'Lifetime expected credit losses' are recognized for the second category. Measurement of the expected credit losses is determined by a probability-weighted estimate of credit losses over the expected life of the financial instrument.

- An asset moves from 12-month expected credit losses to lifetime expected credit losses when there has been a significant deterioration in credit quality since initial recognition. Hence the 'boundary' between 12-month and lifetime losses is based on the change in credit risk not the absolute level of risk at the reporting date.

- There is also an important operational simplification (one of several in the new Standard) that permits companies to stay in '12-month expected credit losses' if the absolute level of credit risk is 'low'. This applies even if the level of credit risk has increased significantly.

Credit losses	Credit losses are defined as the difference between all the contractual cash flows that are due to an entity and the cash flows that it actually expects to receive ('cash shortfalls'). This difference is discounted at the original effective interest rate (or credit-adjusted effective interest rate for purchased or originated credit-impaired financial assets).
12-month expected credit losses	12-month expected credit losses are a portion of the lifetime expected credit losses they are calculated by multiplying the probability of a default occurring on the instrument in the next 12 months by the total (lifetime) expected credit losses that would result from that default they are not the expected cash shortfalls over the next 12 months.
Lifetime expected credit losses	Lifetime expected credit losses are the expected shortfalls in contractual cash flows, taking into account the potential for default at any point during the life of the financial instrument.

Uncollectible Accounts Receivable

An entity may not be able to collect all of its accounts receivable balance. IFRS requires entities to use the allowance method to account for uncollectible receivables. Under the allowance method, entities *estimate* the amount of expected uncollectible accounts. The estimate is recorded as an expense and *reduces accounts receivable through an allowance account*. Collection of accounts receivable previously written off is accounted for similarly under US GAAP and IFRS. The only difference between the two standards relates to terminology. IFRS refers to the allowance accounts as a 'provision.'

Example 4-12 Uncollectible accounts receivable

Muck AG estimates that 3 percent of credit sales will be uncollectible. Muck uses allowance method. Sales are 300,000€. The company will record the following entry.

Debit record	Credit record
Bad debt expense 9,000€	Provision for Bad and Doubtful Debts 9,000€

The provision will be shown on the right side of the balance sheet. The bad debt expense will reduce PL, and consequently it reduces equity, but it will not be credited to the receivable. The receivable will still appear measured at its net realizable value.

At the end of next year, Muck recognizes that 6,000 of the receivables are indeed and finally uncollectible, so they are no longer "doubtful". Now it will write off these uncollectible receivables, and at the same time the provision will be debited.

Debit record	Credit record
Provision for Bad and Doubtful Debts 6,000€	Trade receivables 6,000€

Example 4-13 Comparing IAS 39 and IFRS 9

Muck GmbH is a trading company and has trade receivables at a carrying amount of €500,000 at the balance sheet date 2014. Careful analysis of the receivables reveals:

Debtor A has filed for bankruptcy during 2014. Muck's receivable with Debtor A amounts to €2,200 and Muck expects to recover €0. The time structure, the amounts and the expected credit loss of all the trade receivables is as follows:

Past due (in days)	Amount in €	% of expected credit loss[4]
within maturity	392,200	0.5
1-30 days	52,300	0.8
31-90 days	27,600	5.6
91-180 days	13,200	8.9
180-365 days	7,500	20.3
>365 days	5,000	70.0
Debtor A	2,200	100
Total	500,000	

"Incurred loss model" in IAS 39

IAS 39 requires that the impairment loss has already incurred ("Incurred Loss Model"). Only for Debtor A there is a loss that already incurred being the event of bankruptcy. The expectations concerning all other receivables and their probability of default are irrelevant.

Hence, only the 2,200 receivables against Debtor A will be recognized as a bad debt provision:

---

[4] Estimation is based on past experience.

Debit record	Credit record
Bad debt expense 2,200€	Provision for Bad and Doubtful Debts 2,200€

"Expected loss model" in IFRS 9

Here, expected credit losses are recognized on a timelier basis ("Expected Loss Model") compared to the existing model in IAS 39 (an "incurred loss" model which delays the recognition of credit losses until there is evidence of a credit loss event). An entity will now always recognize (at a minimum) 12-month expected credit losses in profit or loss. Lifetime expected losses will be recognized on assets for which there is a significant increase in credit risk after initial recognition. IFRS 9 provides an exception for the initial recognition of trade receivables without significant financing component to be recognized at the transaction price instead of fair value.

However, Muck GmbH's past experience shows that Muck GmbH can expect 0.5% credit loss on the trade receivables that are totally healthy and performing normally in line with the contractual terms. Muck has estimated the percentages to increase with increasing days that the receivables are overdue. As a result, Muck GmbH needs to recognize bad debt provision based on provision matrix, as this simplification is permitted by IFRS 9.

Bad debt allowance is then calculated as the expected value of the receivables:

$$(392{,}200 \times 0.5\%) + (52{,}300 \times 0.8\%) + (27{,}600 \times 5.6\%) + (13{,}200 \times 8.9\%) + (7{,}500 \times 20.3\%) + (5{,}000 \times 70\%) + (2{,}200 \times 100\%) = 12{,}322.30$$

The total bad debt provision in line with IFRS 9 is €12,322.30.

5   Liabilities

5.1   Provisions and Contingent liabilities (IAS 37)

The liability definition discussed in section 3.3 on page 40 refers just as well to provisions.

IAS 37 *Provisions, Contingent Liabilities and Contingent Assets* uses the term *provision* for a liability of uncertain timing or amount.

- A *Contingent liability* is a possible obligation that arises from past events, whose existence will be confirmed only by the occurrence or non-occurrence of one or more uncertain future events not wholly in the control of the entity; or a present obligation that arises from past events that is not recognized because it is *not probable* that an outflow of resources embodying economic benefits will be required to settle the obligation or the amount of the obligation cannot be measured reliably.

- A *Contingent asset* is a possible asset that arises from past events and whose existence will be confirmed only by the occurrence or non-occurrence of one or more uncertain future events not wholly within the control of the entity.

- A provision is required to be recognized when an outflow of resources to settle the liability is probable and the amount can be reasonably estimated.

- A liability should be recognized using the best estimate of the settlement amount. However, if the entity has a range of estimates that are all equally probable, IFRS recognizes the liability *at the mid-point of the estimates*. IFRS requires the amounts to be updated to the current risk-adjusted discount rate for each financial statement period.

Example 5-1 Asset Retirement Obligation

Muck AG purchases and erects an oil platform at a total cost of 750,000€ at January 1, 2012. The oil platform will be in use for 5 years, at which time the Muck Company is legally obligated to ensure that the platform is dismantled and removed from the site. Muck Company's management estimates that it will have to pay 100,000€ to have the platform dismantled and removed from the site in 5 years. The appropriate interest rate to use in computing the present value of the restoration obligation is 8%. At the end of year 5, Muck AG dismantles the platform at a cost of 150,000€.

Step 1 Determine the present value of the asset retirement obligation

$$PV = 100,000/1.08^5 = 68,058.32€$$

The act of acquiring a long-term operating asset legally obligates the company to incur restoration costs in the future when the asset is retired. The fair value of the obligation is recognized as a liability and is added to the cost of the acquired asset. This would lead to the following journal entries.

Step 2 Recognize both the purchase of the asset and the ARO obligation

Debit record	Credit record
PPE 818,058€	Cash 750,000€
	ARO (Provision) 68,058€

Step 3 Account for the depreciation

The asset will appear in the balance sheet with its cost of 750,000 plus the present value of the estimated cost of retirement. So 818,058€ will be depreciated over useful life of five years, so each year 818,058/5 = 163,612:

Debit record	Credit record
Depreciation 163,612€	Acc Depreciation PPE 163,612€

Step 4 Adjust for the present value of the ARO each year

Each year, Muck has to recognize the *increase* in the present value of the provision using the discount rate of 8 percent. So at the end of the first year, the ARO increases to

$$68,058 \times 1.08 = 73,503€$$

The ARO increases by $68,058 \times 0.08 = 5,445€$. The journal entry is:

Debit record	Credit record
Accretion expense 5,445€	ARO (Provision) 5,445€

Step 5 Full expense schedule and ARO recognition at the end of each year

Over the five years, the expenses resulting from the depreciation and the increase in the ARO liability are:

	t_0	t_1	t_2	t_3	t_4	t_5
PPE depreciation		163,612	163,612	163,612	163,612	163,612
ARO increase	68,058	5,445	5,880	6,351	6,859	7,407
total expenses	~~68,058~~	169,056	169,492	169,962	170,470	171,019
ARO at end of year	68,058	73,503	79,383	85,734	92,593	100,000

The total expense row shows how the purchase of the platform including the retirement obligation is allocated over time. During the five years, the actual amounts are quite similar. This might change bit if the company has to adjust the discount rate they are using. In this simple example this is not assumed to happen.

At the end of the fifth year, the ARO in the balance sheet is 100,000. So if Muck AG has to spend 150,000€ (cash) for the dismantling, the journal entries would be

Debit record	Credit record
ARO (Provision) 100,000€	Cash 150,000€
dismantling expense 50,000€	

Note that the only the 50,000 of the 150,000€ in year 5 decrease profit of year 5, the 100,000€ from the ARO liability have been expensed already over the five years.

5.2   Non-current liabilities

Non-current liabilities are sometimes complex financial instruments that may contain characteristics of both debt and equity. Determining the proper classification of these instruments can be difficult, and the results sometimes differ between the two accounting standards.

Classification of instruments for IFRS, however, focuses on the substance of the transaction. An instrument, or its component parts, should be classified as equity if, and only if, it meets both conditions listed in *IAS 32 Financial Instruments: Presentation.*

(1) The instrument includes no contractual obligation to deliver or exchange cash or financial assets to another entity and

(2) If the instrument will/may be settled in the issuer's own equity instruments it is

a.   a non-derivative that includes no contractual obligation for the issuer to deliver a variable number of its shares or

b.   a derivative that will be settled by the issuer exchanging a fixed amount of cash/other financial assets for a fixed number of its own equity instruments.

Under these rules, *preferred shares* are classified as *equity* if they are not redeemable, or redeemable at the option of the issuer. They are classified as liabilities if they are mandatorily redeemable, redeemable at the option of the shareholder, or contingently redeemable based on future events outside of the control of either party. Puttable instruments, that give the holder the right to put the instrument back to the issuer for cash or another asset, are liabilities.

Convertible debt

A bond that can be exchanged for stock of the company (or other corporate security) at the discretion of the bondholder is a convertible bond. IFRS requires "split accounting" for compound financial instruments whereby the proceeds are allocated between a liability component (at its fair value) and an equity component (the residual amount).

Example 5-2: Convertible Bonds

Muck AG issues 1 million convertible bonds of €1 each paying a nominal coupon interest rate of 10 percent. Bondholders are entitled to convert their bonds into €1 common shares of the company on the date of their maturity in three years' time instead of receiving principal repayment.

The yield to maturity of a similar bond without the conversion option is 15 percent.

The question arises how Muck AG must account for the convertible bonds upon initial recognition, subsequent measurement and maturity assuming all bonds are converted after three years?

Initial Recognition

The liability represented by the bond is the present value of the bond's future cash flows calculated with the YTM 15 percent of the similar bond.

$$PV = \frac{100,000}{1{,}15^1} + \frac{100,000}{1{,}15^2} + \frac{1,100,000}{1{,}15^3} = 885{,}839$$

The difference between the cash issuance of 1,000,000 and the present value of the bond's future cash flow is the value of the option to convert included in the bonds.

Following accounting entries must therefore be recorded upon initial recognition:

Debit record	Credit record
Cash/Bank 1,000,000	Liability 885,839
	Share Options (Equity) 114,161

Subsequent Recognition

Interest expense will be charged using 15 percent. The difference between interest paid and interest charged will be added to the liability component as follows:

	Interest Expense		Liability	
Year 1:	[885,839 x 15%]	132,876	[885,839 + 132,876 – 100,000]	918,715
Year 2:	[918,715 x 15%]	137,807	[918,715+ 137,807 – 100,000]	956,522
Year 3:	[956,522 x 15%]	143,478	[956,522+ 143,478 – 100,000]	1,000,000

The journal entries are:

Year 1:

Debit record	Credit record
Interest expense 132,876	Cash 100,000
	Liability 32,876

Year 2:

Debit record	Credit record
Interest expense 137,807	Cash 100,000
	Liability 37,807

Year 3:

Debit record	Credit record
Interest expense 143,478	Cash 100,000
	Liability 43,478

After year 3, the liability has increased to 1,000,000.

At maturity

If after three years the bondholder exercises his option to convert the bonds into shares the following accounting entry will be required to account for the conversion of bonds into shares after three years:

Debit record	Credit record
Liability 1,000,000	Share Capital 1,000,000
Share Options (Equity) 114,161	Share Premium 114,161

5.3   Income Taxes (IAS 12)

IAS 12 Income Taxes establishes guidelines for the recognition of *deferred taxes* generated by temporary differences between book and taxable income.

Recognition

In IFRS, a deferred tax asset is recognized only if it is probable (more likely than not) that the asset will be applied against future taxable profits.

Calculation

IFRS utilizes tax rates and laws that have been enacted or substantively enacted as of the balance sheet date.

Presentation

For IFRS, deferred tax assets and liabilities are classified as non-current. Supplemental disclosures indicate the nature of each temporary difference and the amounts to be realized within 12 months. US GAAP, however, classifies deferred tax assets and liabilities based on the classification of the related asset or liability. The IASB is expected to release an exposure draft by the end of 2008, conforming the classification of deferred tax assets and liabilities to that of US GAAP.

Revaluation of assets

When property, plant and equipment are revalued for IFRS, this often results in a temporary difference between book and tax bases, as the assets are not revalued for tax purposes. Deferred tax calculated on this difference is recognized directly to equity.

The computation of deferred taxes involves some complexities that are discussed in advanced accounting courses. At this point, you need to understand only that deferred tax assets and liabilities are caused by *temporary differences between the income statement and tax return.* Each temporary difference has an impact on the income statement in one accounting period and on the tax return in another.

Example 5-3 Deferred tax liabilities

Assume that in 2011, Muck AG owned a building that originally cost €10 million. The carrying value (cost less accumulated depreciation) on the balance sheet is €8.5 million. For tax purposes, the book value is €6.5 million. The €2 million difference is caused by using straight-line depreciation for financial reporting and accelerated depreciation for tax purposes. So in this example the depreciation schedule for tax purposes and for the IFRS financial statements are different.

What is the consequence of that? Obviously Muck has already reduced its taxable income in the past because it depreciated more in their tax return than in the IFRS income statement. So the IFRS income statement shows a higher profit than the tax return income statement – which also means Muck paid less taxes according to the tax return than they would have paid if the IFRS income would be subject to taxation (which it is not).

But whatever tax Muck is not paying in the *current* year, they will have to pay in *later* years. Why? Because once the asset is fully depreciated for tax purposes, the full profit (not reduced by any more tax depreciation for that asset) will be subject to taxation, whereas in the IFRS statement there is still some carrying value to depreciate which reduces IFRS income.

The amount of deferred tax liability for 2011 is computed by multiplying the *timing difference* by the corporate tax rate (34%):

$$\textit{Deferred Tax Liability} = \text{€2 million} \times 34\% = \text{€680,000}$$

If there were no other deferred tax items, Muck would report a *deferred tax liability* on its balance sheet of €680,000. These €680,000 liabilities indicate how much Muck still expects to pay in taxes in future periods as of the balance sheet date.

At the end of the following year, 2012, Muck would again compare the tax book value and the IFRS carrying value of the building. Assume that the tax book value of the building was €6 million and the IFRS carrying value was €8.2 million. The timing difference at the end of 2012 would be €2.2 million, resulting in a

$$\textit{Deferred tax liability} \; \text{€2.2 million} \times 34\% = \text{€748,000}$$

The income tax expense reported under IFRS is the amount needed to complete a journal entry once the company has computed its income tax payment for the year and the change in its deferred taxes. Based on our example, the **change** in the deferred tax liability for Muck in 2012 was €68,000 (€748,000 – €680,000) – so the liability went up.

Assume the Muck completed its tax return and determined it owed €550,000 in taxes for the year. The company would record the following:

Debit record	Credit record
Income tax expense 618,000€	Deferred tax (liability) 68,000€
	Income tax payable 550,000€

Example 5-4 Deferred tax assets

Muck AG is restructuring its business and will terminate some of the employees. Muck has agreed to pay a termination bonus of 200,000€ to those affected employees. This creates a constructive obligation for which a provision has to be recognized.

Debit record	Credit record
Restructuring expense 200,000€	Restructuring provision 200,000€
Deferred tax asset 68,000€	Tax payable 68,000€

For tax purposes, tax income is 200,000€ higher than IFRS income, because the restructuring expense is an accounting expense, but will not be accepted as an expense reducing taxable income. What is the consequence of that? Obviously Muck has to pay 34 percent taxes on the higher income of 200,000€, which is 68,000€. The 200,000€ that Muck has already treated as an expense in the IFRS income will lead to a tax expense in later years – so Muck has the expectation to pay less taxes in the future.

The amount of deferred tax asset for 2011 is computed by multiplying the *timing difference* by the corporate tax rate (34%):

$$Deferred\ Tax\ Asset = €200,000 \times 34\% = €68,000$$

If there were no other deferred tax items, Muck would report a *deferred tax asset* on its balance sheet of €68,000. This €68,000 asset indicates how much Muck still expects to pay less tax in future periods as of the balance sheet date.

The computation of deferred taxes involves some complexities that are discussed in advanced accounting courses. At this point, you need to understand only that deferred tax assets and liabilities are caused by *temporary differences between the income statement and tax return.* Each temporary difference has an impact on the income statement in one accounting period and on the tax return in another.

5.4   Employee benefits (IAS 19)

The financial statements should show a realistic figure for the costs of employing staff including the costs of a promised pension or any other future benefits which constitute an obligation to the entity. Otherwise, balance sheets would fail to disclose the liability that the company faces in discharging its obligations. The size of the liability that comes with the promised pension benefits is determined by the details of the plan.

The objective of IAS 19 is to prescribe the accounting and disclosure for these employee benefits, requiring an entity to recognize a liability where an employee has provided service and an expense when the entity consumes the economic benefits of employee service.

IAS 19 (2011) does not apply to employee benefits within the scope of IFRS 2 Share-based Payment or the reporting by employee benefit plans.

The majority of the content of IAS 19 addresses post-employment benefits, i.e. requirements that pensions be accounted for under IFRS.

Example 5-5: Short-term benefits

Muck Srl has 50 employees, and all are entitled to three days of paid sick leave each year, which they can carry forward for five years. At the end of the first year, the average unused entitlement accruing during that year is one day per employee. Muck's experience is that all carried forward sick days are used before the end of the five-year period.

Thus, Muck expects that it will pay an additional 50 days of sick pay in a future period (50 employees × 1 unused sick day each), and it recognizes a liability for this amount.

Profit-sharing and bonus payments

An entity recognizes the expected cost of profit-sharing and bonus payments when, and only when, it has a legal or constructive obligation to make such payments as a result of past events and a reliable estimate of the expected obligation can be made.

Example 5-6 Profit sharing plan

Muck Sweets Import AG has a profit-sharing plan under which it pays 5 percent of its net profits to those employees who have worked for the company for all 12 months of the year. Muck retains the profit distribution for any employees who are not still working for the company at the end of the year. Based on its historical 10 percent employee turnover rate, Muck estimates that it will pay out 4.5 percent of its profits, and so it recognizes a liability and expense for that amount.

Types of post-employment benefit plans

Post-employment benefit plans are informal or formal arrangements where an entity provides post-employment benefits to one or more employees, e.g. retirement benefits (pensions or lump sum payments), life insurance and medical care.

The accounting treatment for a post-employment benefit plan depends *on the economic substance of the plan* and results in the plan being classified as either a defined contribution plan or a defined benefit plan:

Feature	Defined contribution plans	Defined benefit plans
Definition	Under a defined contribution plan, *the entity pays fixed contributions into a fund* but has no legal or constructive obligation to make further payments if the fund does not have sufficient assets to pay all of the employees' entitlements to post-employment benefits. The entity's obligation is therefore effectively limited to the amount it agrees to contribute to the fund and *effectively places actuarial and investment risk on the employee.*	Under a defined benefit scheme the retirement benefits are determined, sometimes on the basis of average salary over the employee's period of service, but more often on the basis of salary in the final year or years before retirement. These plans create an obligation on the entity to provide agreed benefits to current and past employees and effectively places actuarial and investment risk on the entity. The pensions payable depend on such factors as the future rate of increase in wages and salaries and the life expectancy of pensioners and, where relevant, their dependents. In addition, the cost in the year of providing future pensions depends upon the rate of return to be earned on contributions and reinvested receipts.

Recognition of defined contribution plan

In a defined contribution plan, the contributions (e.g. to a pension fund) are recognized *as an expense in the period in which they are incurred.*

If the employer matches the amount and timing of his contributions to obligations for each accounting period, *it is not necessary to recognize further liabilities.*

The balance sheet is impacted by defined contribution plans only *if the company has not matched the timing and amount of its contributions to obligations during the accounting period*:

- A liability is incurred when the plan is under-funded, i.e. the amount paid is lower than the contributions due (deferred liability).

- An asset is recognized when the plan is over-funded, i.e. the amount paid is greater than the contributions due (prepaid expense). Once a company's commitment to (matching) contribution payments has been fulfilled, no further consideration regarding the recognition of liabilities is necessary.

- Contributions are paid to a legally separate entity. This entity is exclusively responsible for the future payments to beneficiaries. The company itself no longer has access to the plan assets after payment of the contributions.

- The company is then no longer to be considered the legal or economic beneficiary of the assets, which are attributable to the eligible employees and are not to be recognized on the balance sheet of the company.

Measurement of a Defined benefit plan

- *Benefit estimation.* Use actuarial methods to estimate the amount of employee benefits *earned* in the current and prior periods. This requires the use of demographic variables, such as employee turnover and mortality, as well as financial variables, such as future changes in salaries and medical costs, that influence benefit costs.

- *Discounting.* Discount the resulting benefit using the projected unit credit method. This results in the present value of the obligation, as well as the current service cost. The central economic assumption is the *discount rate* at which future benefits are discounted to the valuation date.

- *Fair value.* Determine the fair value of any plan assets. With the revised version of IAS 19 rev. 2011 published on 16 June 2011, the return on plan assets ("expected return on plan assets" in the terminology prior to IAS 19 rev. 2011) was substantially revised. *For accounting periods starting from 1 January 2013, the applicable discount rate for the calculation of the pension obligation is implicitly used as return rate for the plan assets as well.* Accordingly, the return on plan assets will no longer be determined individually for the company, and the allocation of the plan assets is irrelevant to its determination.

- *Gains and losses.* Determine total gains and losses, as well as the amount of those actuarial gains and losses that can be recognized.

- *Past service cost.* If the plan has been introduced or changed, calculate the past service cost.

- *Settlement cost.* If the plan has been curtailed or settled, calculate the resulting gain or loss.

Actuarial assumptions used in measurement

The overall actuarial assumptions used must be unbiased and mutually compatible, and represent the best estimate of the variables determining the ultimate post-employment benefit cost.

- Financial assumptions must be based on market expectations at the end of the reporting period.

- Mortality assumptions are determined by reference to the best estimate of the mortality of plan members during and after employment. The most important parameters for demographic assessment are the probabilities for the occurrence of the biometric risks of death and disability. Although these probabilities could, in principle, be determined individually for each set of people to be assessed, due to insufficient set size and excessive cost, statistical analyses are usually based on generally accepted actuarial tables for probabilities of death and disability. In Germany, the so-called Heubeck actuarial tables are customarily used for IFRS accounting of pension liabilities. These actuarial tables can also be customized for an individual company by applying modifications (increase or reduction of probabilities).

- The discount rate should, in principle, reflect the time value of money and be based on the yields of high quality fixed-income corporate bonds on the valuation date. In practice, "high quality corporate bonds" usually means corporate bonds rated at least AA (using the terminology of Standard & Poor's). The maturity and currency of the bonds and the pension obligation should also match. Since the introduction of the Eurozone, there has generally been a sufficiently liquid market for corporate bonds denominated in Euro to determine the discount rate. If, however, there is no sufficiently liquid market for such corporate bonds, the market yield on government bonds may be used alternatively (taking into account a risk premium to compensate for the difference in credit quality). If there is no sufficiently active market for very long-term bonds (which is a particular issue for maturities longer than 30 years), the discount rate is derived using mathematical extrapolation methods.

- Assumptions about expected salaries and benefits reflect the terms of the plan, future salary increases, any limits on the employer's share of cost, contributions from employees or third parties*, and estimated future changes in state benefits that impact benefits payable

- Medical cost assumptions incorporate future changes resulting from inflation and specific changes in medical costs

Projected Unit Credit Method

Under IAS 19, since 31 December 1999, the Projected Unit Credit Method (PUC method) has been explicitly required as the actuarial valuation method for the IFRS balance sheet. The Projected Unit Credit Method is a valuation procedure from the aggregation methods class.

Under aggregation methods, the amount of the pension obligation is calculated as the sum of the expected future benefit payments discounted on the respective closing dates and weighted with their probabilities, provided they have been accrued by the reporting date. Based on the individual obligation resulting from a classic defined benefit plan, the premium required to fund the pension obligation increases over time, as the discount period continues to shorten. A particular characteristic of the Projected Unit Credit Method is that the value of the pension claims on each reporting date is not based on reporting date assumptions, but instead is anticipated or determined (hence „projected") by taking into account future changes of the key valuation parameters, such as salary and pension trends.

Using the the 'projected unit credit method' also means, that the present value of an entity's defined benefit obligations and related service costs sees *each period of service as giving rise to an additional unit of benefit entitlement and measures each unit separately in building up the final obligation.*

This requires an entity to attribute benefit to the current period (to determine current service cost) and the current and prior periods (to determine the present value of defined benefit obligations). Benefit is attributed to periods of service using the plan's benefit formula, unless an employee's service in later years will lead to a materially higher of benefit than in earlier years, in which case a straight-line basis is used.

The fair value of any plan assets is deducted from the present value of the defined benefit obligation in determining the net deficit or surplus. The determination of the net defined benefit liability (or asset) is carried out with sufficient regularity such that the amounts recognized in the financial statements do not differ materially from those that would be determined at end of the reporting period.

Pension Expense

Pension expense will include Service cost, Net interest and Remeasurement.

Service Cost

Service cost will be recognized in profit and loss and calculated prospectively by the actuary. It includes:

- Current service cost
- Past service cost and
- Settlements.

The *current service cost* corresponds to the actuarial cash value of the benefit components that are newly accrued by the (active) employees during the accounting period. Analogous to the defined benefit obligation, the following applies: All other things being equal, a higher discount rate reduces current service cost, and a lower discount rate increases current service cost.

Past service cost may result from the subsequent improvement or deterioration of a pension plan. Unlike original current service cost, which reflects the benefit components newly accrued in the current accounting period, past service cost *always relates to previous accounting periods*.

With a *settlement*, the company transfers, without any extended liability, the pension obligation for which it is responsible to another entity (e. g. another company or pension provider), or the pension obligation is extinguished by the payment of a termination indemnity. In accordance with IAS 19.113, the conclusion of an insurance contract does not lead to a settlement, if the employer remains subject to the extended liability to pay benefits.

Net Interest

Net interest, which is also recognized in profit and loss, represents the interest income or expense resulting from the net liability or from the net assets (so-called net defined benefit liability / asset as the difference between pension obligations and plan assets). Under IAS 19 rev. 2011 the discount rate used to calculate the benefit obligation is now to be applied to both figures, the plan assets and the benefit liability. Expected changes during the accounting period due to pension payments or funding of plan assets are taken into account. A simple mathematical expression of net interest is:

$$\text{Net interest} = (\text{plan assets} - \text{pension obligation}) \times \text{discount rate}$$

Remeasurement

At the end of the accounting period, deviations naturally occur between the prospectively measured values (i.e. the expected values) and the actual values for the pension obligation, plan assets, etc. The reasons for this can, for example, be found in changed discount rates, the occurrence of biometric risks or unexpected developments of plan assets. These discrepancies between the expected and actual values are referred to as remeasurement.

The valuation changes basically include all the changes in the pension obligation and the fair value of plan assets, as far as these are not included in service cost or net interest, i.e. they include in particular:

- actuarial gains and losses on the liability side (e. g. conditioned by changes in the discount rate) and

- deviations in the actual development of plan assets from the corresponding part of the net interest allocated to plan assets (based on the discount rate).

In contrast to the recognition of service cost and net interest in the profit and loss statement, the remeasurement is immediately and completely recorded in equity, specifically in the statement of comprehensive income in accordance with IAS 1.81 (other comprehensive income (OCI)). There is no longer any provision for deferred recognition in income of these amounts, such as in the framework of the corridor method, which was done away with in IAS 19 rev. 2011.

The recognition of the remeasurement in other comprehensive income protects the income statement from excessive volatility. This approach is, in practice, often referred to as OCI, an approach that has been in the standard since 2004, and which had already been applied in Germany before the introduction of IAS 19 rev. 2011. It has been used by about two-thirds of DAX companies and has found broad acceptance.

Elimination of Corridor Approach

IASB has eliminated the corridor approach previously allowed by IAS 19. Companies will be required to recognize all changes in the fair value of plan assets and defined benefit obligations in the period in which they occur. Return on assets will be reported in total, rather than dividing the return into its current components – expected return and actuarial gains/losses.

Example 5-7 Defined Benefit Plan – Measurement

At the end of 2014, the employment contract of 40-year old Karl Kaputnik, chief engineer of the Muck Corporation, has been amended for retirement benefits. Relevant data is as follows:

- According to the amendment, he will receive a pension upon his retirement from Muck, at the age of 67. The retirement pension is calculated to be 1.5 percent of Kaputnik's final annual salary for each year that he has been working for the Muck Corporation until retirement.

- At the end of 2014, Kaputnik has already been working 5 years for the Muck Corporation.
- Kaputnik has an annual salary of 55,000€ now, which is expected to grow until retirement with a growth rate of 3 percent each year.
- Life expectancy for Karl Kaputnik according to relevant life tables after reaching his retirement age of 67 is 18 years.
- For simplicity, let us assume that all pensions payments will be fully vested, and payments will be made at the end of each year. The Muck Corporation uses a 4 percent discount rate to measure the pension liabilities.
- All calculated figures rounded, but we will not round the present or future value factors – so there will be some rounding errors.

Step 1: Determine the future salary on which the pension will be based

At his age of retirement, he will earn a salary of

$$55{,}000 \times 1.03^{27} = 122{,}171€.$$

Step 2: Determine the pension based on the future salary considering the years of service

At year-end 2014, he has worked for the company already 5 years, so his expected annual pension which he has "earned" by working 5 years already is

$$122{,}171 \times 5 \times 0.015 = 9{,}163€.$$

Step 3: Determine the present value (PV) on retirement of the pension payments

The annual pension – still based on 5 years of working for the company – would be paid for the life expectancy of 18 years. The present value of these 18 payments at the beginning of retirement (year 2041) is

$$9{,}163 \times PVAF(18yrs;4\%) = 9{,}163 \times 12.65929697 = 115{,}995€$$

115,995€ is the theoretical capital that has to be available so that an annuity of 9,163 can be paid out annually for 18 times, if the remaining capital still earns 4 percent each year.

Step 4: Determine the PV of the pension payments at end of the accounting period 2014

The present value of the 115,995€ at the end of 2014 is

$$115{,}995/1.04^{27} = 40{,}229€.$$

The future obligation at time of retirement has a present value at the end of 2014 (=beginning of 2015) of 40,229€. In other words: a hypothetical capital of 40,229€ would have to earn 4 percent each year for the next 27 years to grow to 115,995€.

Step 5: Determine how the above numbers change if Kaputnik worked an additional year

To see the effect of what happens to the obligation during the accounting period, we have to calculate the effect of Kaputnik working one additional year. Accordingly, numbers above have to be recalculated.

- At the end of 2015, he has worked for the company already 6 years, so his expected annual pension which he has "earned" by working 6 years is:

$$122{,}171 \times 6 \times 0.015 = 10{,}995 \text{€}.$$

- This annual pension – still from the perspective of 6 years work – would be paid for the life expectancy of 18 years. The present value of these 18 payments at the beginning of retirement (year 2041) is

$$10{,}995 \times \text{PVAF}(18\text{yrs};4\%) = 10{,}995 \times 12.65929697 = 139{,}194 \text{€}.$$

- 139,194€ is the theoretical capital that has to be available so that an annuity of 10,995 can be paid out annually for 18 times, if the remaining capital still earns 4 percent each year.

- The present value of the 139,194€ at the end of 2015 is $139{,}194/1{,}04^{26} = 50{,}206 \text{€}$ (now only discounted for 26 years, because from year end 2015 to 2041, it is only 26 years to go).

- The present value of the future obligation at the end of 2015 (=beginning of 2016) is therefore grown to 50,206€.

Step 6: Allocate the increase of the obligation on service cost and interest cost

The increase in the Projected Benefit Obligation at the end of 2015 is 50,206 – 40,229 = 9,977€. This increase is to be divided into interest cost and service cost.

- The interest cost for the PBO is $40{,}229 \times 0.04 = 1{,}609 \text{€}$.

- The service cost is therefore $9{,}977 - 1{,}609 = 8{,}368 \text{€}$.

The PBO is a liability that the company has towards the employee. Cum grano salis we can say the employee has agreed to defer the receipt of some of his compensation, so it is something like a loan to the company. The charge on this loan comes in the form of interest to be paid. But the interest is not paid, instead the interest of 1,609€ is added to the "principal" of 40,229€.

But the obligation has increased even more, namely by an additional 8,368€. These represent the increase in value because the employee has worked an additional year. This additional year of work increases the employee's future pension payments, and consequently increases the present value of the obligation. Both – interest cost and service cost – are expenses being recognized in profit and loss.

6   Ownership interest

6.1   Earnings per share (IAS 33)

Disclosures

Under IFRS accounting, firms are required to disclose earnings per share information on the face of the income statement if their common stock is publicly traded, or if they are in the process of issuing stock for public trade. Required disclosures include both basic and diluted calculations of per share income from continuing operations and net profit or loss.

Diluted earnings per share

- *Incremental shares* – The treasury stock method is used to calculate diluted EPS. IFRS calculates incremental shares using a weighted average at the end of the year (rather than on a quarterly basis for example).

- *Contracts settled in cash or shares* – IFRS assumes the contract will be settled in shares, and it should be included in diluted earnings per share if the impact is dilutive.

Table 6-1: Various scenarios for the calculation of EPS

Scenario	Description	Example No. Page
EPS – Basic case	The company does not have any potential new common shares which might be issued or otherwise created. If no other securities than common stock are issued (no preferred stock) and the number of common shares remains unchanged during the period, only basic EPS will be reported.	Example 6-1 Page 132
Issuance of new shares	New shares being issued during the period will be time-weighted by the fraction of the period they were outstanding. So if 10 million new shares were issued July 1, they would be issued only for half a year, hence it would be assumed 10 million x 0.5 = 5 million have been issued on the average all year.	Example 6-2 Page 132
Stock dividend, Stock split	A stock dividend of 10% means that stockholders get 10 new shares for any 100 they are holding. A stock split of 3-for-2 means that any 2 shares outstanding will be replaced by 3 shares, so that the number of shares will increase by 50 percent. Economically both are the same: the number of stock increases, the An increase of shares coming from a stock dividend (or from a stock split) is not time-weighted.	Example 6-3 Page 133

Scenario	Description	Example No. Page
Treasury stock	If common stocks are reacquired from owners and kept by the company (treasury stock), these shares are time-weighted for the fraction of the period they were not outstanding (which means for the period of time the company owns them). Since the company has not rights from these shares, no profit is earned on these shares – nobody can claim any profit allocated on these shares. Therefore the time-weighted shares are subtracted from the shares in the denominator, since they are not part of the shares earning profit.	Example 6-4 Page 133
EPS for common shareholders after preferred dividends	Any dividend paid to preferred stockholders is subtracted from net income – it decreases the earnings for the common shareholders – hence it decreases EPS. And since the denominator in the EPS calculation is the weighted average number of common shares, the numerator should reflect appropriately the earnings available to common shareholders only.	Example 6-5 Page 134
(Employee) stock options	Any stock options (also stock rights and stock warrants) give the holder the right to buy a specified number of shares and pay a predetermined price for these shares (exercise price) once the option is free to be exercised. If at the time the option may be exercised, the market price of the stock is higher than the exercise price (option is "in the money") it makes sense to exercise the option and buy the stock for the lower exercise price and enjoying the higher market value of the stock. For calculating EPS it is pretended that the option has been exercised at the beginning of the period (!), provided it was "in the money" based on the average market price of the shares. Then it is pretended as if the company bought back shares with the proceeds from the exercise – and any shares not bought back are assumed to be issued fresh, thus increasing the number of outstanding shares.	Example 6-6 Page 134
Convertible bonds	Similar to the options for the calculation of diluted EPS it is pretended that the convertible bonds have been converted at the beginning of the period. Since the net income has been decreased by the interest expense incurred by the bonds, for the diluted EPS the earnings figure in the numerator is increased by the after-tax interest that would have been avoided in the event of conversion.	Example 6-7 Page 135

Example 6-1: Earnings per share – Basic case

In the most basic setting, earnings per share is simply a company's earnings (or loss) divided by the number of shares outstanding.

Muck AG reported net income of €154 million in 2014. Its tax rate was 40%.

> Common stock outstanding on January 1, 2014: 60 million shares
>
> Basic EPS:

$$EPS = \frac{net\ income\ 154m}{60m\ shares} = 2.57€\ /\ share$$

Example 6-2: Earnings per share – Issuance of new shares

Muck AG reported net income of €154 million for 2014 (tax rate 40%). Its capital structure included:

> Common stock outstanding on January 1: 60 million common shares
>
> On March 1: 12 million new shares were sold to investors
>
> Basic EPS:

$$EPS = \frac{net\ income\ 154m}{60m\ shares + 12m \times \dfrac{10}{12}} = 2.20€\ /\ share$$

If the number of shares has changed, the denominator is the *weighted average* of the shares outstanding during the period the earnings were generated. Any new shares issued are time-weighted by the fraction of the period they were outstanding and then added to the number of shares outstanding for the entire period. The new shares have been sold as of March 1 – so the new shares are outstanding for 10 of 12 months of the year. "Time weighted" means the 12 million new shares are multiplied with $10/12 = 0.833$. In a way this is like saying 12 million (new) shares outstanding for 10 months is like $12 \times 0.833 = 10$ million shares outstanding on average for the entire year.

Stock split and stock dividends

- A capitalization or bonus issue (sometimes referred to as a **stock dividend**) is the issue of new shares to shareholders *in proportion to their existing holdings*.

- A share split (sometimes referred to as a **stock split**) is the dividing of an entity's existing shares into multiple shares. For example, in a share split, each shareholder may receive nine additional shares for each share held. The result is that the entity has

- In some cases, the previously outstanding shares are cancelled and replaced by new shares. Capitalization and bonus issues and share splits do not change total equity. An entity shall reclassify amounts within equity as required by applicable laws.

Example 6-3: Earnings per share – Stock dividend

Muck AG reported net income of €154 million in 2014 (tax rate 40%). Its capital structure included:

Common stock outstanding as of January 1: 60 million common shares

On March 1: 12 million new shares were sold

On June 17: a 10 percent stock dividend was distributed

Basic EPS:

$$EPS = \frac{net\ income\ 154m}{60m\ shares \times 1.1 + 12m \times \dfrac{10}{12} \times 1.1} = \frac{154}{77} = 2.00€\ /\ share$$

The additional shares created by a stock dividend or split are **not** weighted for the time period they were outstanding. Shares outstanding prior to the stock distribution are retroactively restated to reflect the increase in shares – that is, treated as if the distribution occurred at the beginning of the period. Therefore, any number of shares existing will be multiplied by the factor representing the increase in the share base – here with 1.1, since the shares have been increased by the stock dividends by 10 percent.

Example 6-4: Earnings per share – Treasury stock

Muck AG reported net income of €154 million in 2014 (tax rate 40%). Its capital structure included:

Common stock outstanding as of January 1: 60 million common shares

On March 1: 12 million new shares were sold

On June 17: a 10 percent stock dividend was distributed

On October 1: 8 million shares were reacquired as treasury stock

Basic EPS:

$$EPS = \frac{net\ income\ 154m}{60m\ shares \times 1.1 + 12m \times \dfrac{10}{12} \times 1.1 - 8 \times \dfrac{3}{12}} = \frac{154}{75} = 2.05€\ /\ share$$

The stock dividend adjustment (the increase of the number of shares by 10 percent) is not necessary for the treasury shares since they were reacquired after the stock dividend. Though the company holds the reacquired shares, a company owning its own shares cannot exercise any rights from these shares (other than selling them or giving them to third parties). The number of reacquired shares is time-weighted for the fraction of the year they were not outstanding (which is 3 months from 12), prior to being subtracted from the number of shares outstanding.

Preferred dividends and earnings available to common shareholders

Preferred dividends are subtracted from net income so that "earnings available to common shareholders" is divided by the weighted average number of common shares.

Example 6-5: Earnings per share – EPS for common shareholders after preferred dividends

Muck AG reported net income of €154 million in 2014 (tax rate 40%). Its capital structure included:

> Common stock outstanding on January 1: 60 million common shares
>
> March 1   12 million new shares were sold
>
> June 17   A 10% stock dividend was distributed
>
> October 1   8 million shares were reacquired as treasury stock
>
> Preferred stock, non-convertible shares, Jan. 1- Dec. 31, 5 million 8% €10 par

Basic EPS:

Each preferred share earns 8 percent on the par value of €10, and since there are 5 million preferred shares outstanding, the preferred shareholders will get in total a 0.08 × 10 × 5m = 4 million Euros, which are subtracted from net income. Only 150 million are available to common shareholders after preferred shareholders claims have been considered. The EPS is then calculated:

$$EPS = \frac{net\ income\ 154m - 4m\ (\text{preferred div.})}{60m\ shares \times 1.1 + 12m \times \dfrac{10}{12} \times 1.1 - 8 \times \dfrac{3}{12}} = \frac{150}{75} = 2.00$$

Calculation of diluted EPS

Diluted EPS incorporates the dilutive effect of potential common shares. The dilutive effect is included essentially by "pretending" the securities already have been exercised, converted, or otherwise transformed into common shares.

Example 6-6: Diluted EPS – Employee stock options

The basic data is taken from Example 6-5.

In addition to the scenario in that example, executive stock options have been granted in 2012. The options are exercisable after 2013 for 15 million common shares (adjusted for the stock dividends) at an exercise price of €20 per share. The average market price of the stock was €25.

The options have a dilutive effect because the average market price (€25) is greater than the exercise price (€20), so hypothetically it would make sense to exercise them. Under the treasury stock approach, the EPS is calculated as if the options were exercised. If the options were exercised, the company would receive the exercise price, which is 15,000,000 options x €20 exercise price = €300 million.

Therefore, Muck AG will issue 15 million shares, but acquire only 12 million shares (€300 million proceeds from exercising the options ÷ €25 per share average market price = 12 million shares). This calculation can be interpreted as if the money the company receives (theoretically) from exercising the options is only good for acquiring 12 million shares – 3 million will still have to be issued newly by the company which is reflected in the denominator.

Therefore, the denominator of the earnings per share formula will increase and earnings per share will decrease.

$$EPS = \frac{net\ income\ 154m - 4m\ (\text{preferred div.})}{60m\ shares \times 1.1 + 12m \times \dfrac{10}{12} \times 1.1 - 8 \times \dfrac{3}{12} + 3} = \frac{150}{78} = 1.92$$

Example 6-7: Convertible bonds

An even more complex scenario is given in case Muck AG had issued convertible bonds in addition to the other capital structure decisions. Convertible bonds are bonds that contain the additional right to the bond holder to convert the bonds into stock of the company.

For diluted EPS, the conversion into common stock is assumed to have occurred at the beginning of the period. The denominator of the EPS fraction is increased by the additional amount of common shares that would have been issued upon conversion.

The numerator is adjusted for the after-tax interest or preferred dividends that would have not been paid by the company if the convertible securities were already converted.

Muck AG reported net income of €154 million in 2014 (tax rate 40%). Its capital structure included:

   Common stock outstanding on January 1: 60 million common shares

   March 1   12 million new shares were sold

   June 17   A 10% stock dividend was distributed

   October 1   8 million shares were reacquired as treasury stock

   Preferred stock, non-convertible shares, Jan. 1- Dec. 31, 5 million 8% on €10 par

   Executive stock options have been granted in 2012, exercisable after 2013 for 15 million common shares (adjusted for the stock dividends) at an exercise price of €20 per share. The average market price of the stock was €25.

   Convertible bonds, coupon interest 10% at €300 million face amount issued in 2013, convertible into 12 million common shares (adjusted for the stock dividend).

The calculation assumes the bonds have been converted as of the beginning of the period (therefore the 12 in the denominator), and therefore the net income is increased by the after-tax interest on the bonds, which would not have been paid by the company, had the bonds been converted:

$$EPS = \frac{net\ income\ 154m - 4m\ (\text{preferred div.}) + 30m - (0.4 \times 30m)}{60m\ shares \times 1.1 + 12m \times \dfrac{10}{12} \times 1.1 - 8 \times \dfrac{3}{12} + 3 + 12} = \frac{168}{90} = 1.92$$

6.2   Share-Based Compensation IFRS 2

IFRS 2 Share-Based Payment is about reporting of employee share plans, awards by shareholders, and cash bonuses. For IFRS these plans are treated in the same manner as other share-based compensation transactions. IFRS 2 is applicable to transactions in which a shareholder of the company uses an equity instrument to compensate a third party for goods/services provided to the company.

A share-based payment arrangement is a contract between the entity (or shareholders of the entity) and another party (including an employee) that entitles the other party to receive

- cash or other assets of the entity for amounts that are based on the price (or value) of equity instruments (including shares or share options) of the entity or another group entity; or

- equity instruments (including shares or share options) of the entity or another group entity, provided the specified vesting conditions, if any, are met.

Classification of awards

IFRS recognizes two classes of share-based compensation. Equity-settled transactions occur when a company enters into an agreement to acquire goods and/or services in exchange for shares of its stock (or other equity instruments). These transactions are recorded at the fair value of the services received. When shares are used to compensate employees, the fair value is determined using the market value of the stock. Cash-settled transactions occur when a company enters into an agreement in which it incurs a liability linked to the company's stock price. These liabilities are typically settled by the transfer of cash or other assets. Equity-settled transactions are recorded at the grant date. Cash-settled transactions are recorded at the grant date, but re-measured to fair value in each period until the liability is settled.

If the agreement provides an option for settlement by equity shares or cash, IFRS requires the award be separated into separate components for cash-settled (to the extent any liability is expected to be settled in cash or other assets) and equity-settled (the excess of the transaction's fair value over the liability incurred).

If an agreement specifies a fixed amount (such as a 5,000€ bonus) to be settled in a variable number of shares (5,000€/share price at the settlement date) IFRS classifies the amount in equity due to its settlement method.

Grant date

IFRS defines the grant date as the time at which the two parties come to an agreement on the terms and conditions of the arrangement.

Recognition

Under IFRS, awards are recognized over the related period of employee service. IFRS does not include the concept of derived service period.

Recognition of awards with graded vesting (e.g. a company awards 100,000 share options vesting 50% the first year, 30% the second year and 20% the third year). IFRS requires the company to account for each separately vesting amount, as if the company made three separate awards.

Taxes

Under IFRS, both payroll and income taxes are recognized at the same time as the compensation expense, and will be accrued over time. Under IFRS, a deferred tax asset is recognized when share options have current intrinsic value. Adjustments, primarily recognized in the income statement, are made to the deferred tax asset each reporting period based on the current market value of the stock.

Example 6-8 Share-based compensation with only service condition

1. Base case

An entity grants 100 share options (with a fair value of 15€ each) to each of its 500 employees, conditional upon the employee working for the next three years. Management estimates that 20 percent of the employees will nevertheless leave the company within the next three years, so that they will lose their rights to the share options. Calculation of the total expense is:

500 employees ×100 share options × 0.8 × 15€ = 600,000€.

The total expected value of what is going to be earned by employees is 600,000€ – but it is going to be earned over three years. So each year 600,000/3 = 200,000€ is being expensed.

Under IFRS 2, an entity only recognizes compensation expense for options with non-market performance conditions if such awards ultimately vest. Therefore the company has to estimate how many employees will forfeit the awards.

2. Change of estimates

Year	Employees actually leaving	Estimates of total employee departure are revised for this year to
1	20	15 percent
2	22	12 percent
3	15	

Year	Calculation	Period expense	Cumulative expense
1	50,000 options × 0.85 × 15€ × 1/3 years	212,500	212,500
2	(50,000 options × 0.88 × 15€ × 2/3 years) − 212,500	227,500	440,000
3	(44,300 options × 15€) − 440,000	224,500	664,500

By year 3, 57 employees of 500 have actually left the company, so only 443 employees will receive options – in total 44,300 options. The period expense is at each year the estimated number of options to be used multiplied with the fair value of the option, and allocated on 1 year.

6.3   Equity

Equity is the residual interest in the assets of the company after deducting all liabilities. Equity is often referred to as shareholders' equity, stockholders' equity, or corporate capital. Equity is often divided on the statement of financial position into the following categories.

(1) Share capital.

(2) Share premium.

(3) Retained earnings.

(4) Accumulated other comprehensive income.

(5) Treasury shares.

(6) Non-controlling interest (minority interest).

Companies have to make a distinction between contributed capital (paid-in capital) and earned capital.

- Contributed capital (paid-in capital) is the total amount paid in on capital shares – the amount provided by shareholders to the corporation for use in the business. Contributed capital includes items such as the par value of all outstanding shares and premiums less discounts on issuance.

- Earned capital is the capital that develops from profitable operations. It consists of all undistributed profits that remain invested in the company. Retained earnings represent the earned capital of the company.

Equity is a residual interest and therefore its value is derived from the amount of the corporations' assets and liabilities. Only in unusual cases will a company's equity equal the total fair value of its shares.

Example 6-9: Equity Hugo Boss AG

Hugo Boss AG recently had total group equity of €860 million (€70.4 million of which is subscribed capital with a par value of 1€ for each ordinary share) and a market capitalization of around €3,850 million (March 2016) – the market value of equity was almost 4.5 times the book value of equity.

Hugo Boss' equity represents the net contributions from shareholders (from both majority and minority shareholders) plus retained earnings (around €800 million) and accumulated other comprehensive income (around €14.7 million). As a residual interest, its equity has no existence apart from the assets and liabilities of Hugo Boss – equity equals net assets. Equity is not a claim to specific assets but a claim against a portion of the total assets. Its amount is not specified or fixed; it depends on the company's profitability. Equity grows if it is profitable. It shrinks, or may disappear entirely, if the company loses value.

In accordance with IAS 1, all changes in equity from transactions with owners are to be presented separately from non-owner changes in equity. IAS 1 requires an entity to present a statement of changes in equity including the following components on the face of the statement:

(1) Total comprehensive income for the period, segregating amounts attributable to owners and to minority interest;

(2) The effects of retrospective application or retrospective restatement in accordance with IAS 8, separately for each component of equity;

(3) Contributions from and distributions to owners; and

(4) Reconciliation between the carrying amount at the beginning and the end of the period, separately disclosing each change, for each component of equity.

The amount of dividends recognized as distributions to equity holders during the period, and the related amount per share should be presented either on the face of the statement of changes in equity or in the notes.

According to IAS 1, except for changes resulting from transactions with owners (such as equity contributions, re-acquisitions of the entity's own equity instruments, dividends, and costs related to these transactions with owners), the change in equity during the period represents the total amount of income and expense (including gains and losses) arising from activities other than those with owners.

Example 6-10: Function of Share premium

One function of additionally paid-in capital (share premium) is to visualize the separation of the equity representing the voting and profit rights from the equity that was contributed by owners for which no voting or profit rights have been obtained by the shareholders. A typical case may occur if a company issues additional stocks for new shareholders. As an illustration, let us assume that two business partners A and B found a stock corporation (a German AG or Aktiengesellschaft), after which they take a third partner into the company.

Step 1: Founding of the company by shareholders A and B

A and B invest €50,000 and found the AB Corporation. They decide to issue 100,000 shares of stock with a par value of €1 and pay the contribution in full on the company's bank account. Now A and B together own 50,000 shares of the AB Corporation. The journal entry for this is:

Debit record	Credit record
Cash 100,000€	Common stock (Issued stock) 100,000€

Step 2: Issuing new shares for additional capital injections by new shareholders

A and B have aggressive business ideas and want to take the next step of expansion. To finance the ideas they want to raise additional capital in the amount of €10 million. They start negotiations with venture capitalist C. C is convinced of the business idea and is willing to invest the €10 million. A and B are willing to cede 40 percent of the company for the €10 million investment. After some negotiations, C finally agrees to invest €10 million for 40 percent of the company's shares.

Technically, if A and B want C to own 40 percent of the shares after the issuance of the new shares, A and B will need to hold 60 percent of the shares. So their 100,000 shares have to represent 60 percent of the shares. 100 percent therefore would be 100,000/0.6 = 166,667 shares. Hence, the number of new shares to be issued is 66,667. For the €10 million C receives (only) 66,667 shares. The difference of €10,000,000 – 66,667 = €9,933,333 is the premium C has to pay – the *additional paid-in capital*.

The journal entry after the issuance of the new shares:

Debit record	Credit record
Cash 10,000,000€	Common stock (Issued stock) 66,667€
	Share premium 9,933,333€

For €66,667 investor C has received voting and profit rights – C now owns 40 percent of the company's shares. The share premium (additional paid-in capital) of €9,933,333 actually buys the new owner nothing – except the opportunity to be part of the company.

Accounting students have to understand the financial side of a stock issuance. The existing shareholders finally decide on the terms for which new shares are being issued. And the number of ownership rights being granted is separated from the capital that is to be contributed by the new shareholders – and that separation can be seen in the balance sheet in equity.

Example 6-11: Treasury shares

Muck AG had the following equity accounts on January 1, 2014:

>   Share Capital – Ordinary: (€1 par) €400,000;

>   Additional paid-in capital (share premium) – ordinary €500,000;

>   Retained Earnings €100,000

In 2014, €60,000 net income was reported, and the company had the following treasury share transactions during the year:

>   Mar 1   Purchased 5,000 shares at €7 per share.

>   June 1 Sold 1,000 shares at €10 per share.

>   Sep 1   Sold 2,000 shares at €9 per share.

>   Dec 1   Sold 1,000 shares at €5 per share.

Thus, the Equity section for Muck AG at December 31, 2014 may look like this:

in €

Subscribed capital (ordinary)	400,000
Own shares (treasury stock)	(7,000)
Share premium (capital reserve)	505,000
Retained earnings	160,000
Total equity	1,058,000

The treasury stock is simply subtracted from equity and the securities repurchased will not be shown on the asset side of the balance sheet. Treasury shares are no real assets, as the company cannot assume any rights from these shares (no voting rights, no profit rights). The journal entries for these transactions would be:

Date	Debit record	Credit record
March 1	Own shares (equity) 35,000	Cash 35,000
June 1	Cash 10,000	Own shares (equity) 7,000 Share premium 3,000
Sept 1	Cash 18,000	Own shares (equity) 14,000 Share premium 4,000
Dec 1	Cash 5,000 Share premium 2,000	Own shares (equity) 7,000

Calculation of treasury shares

Date of transaction	no of shares bought (+) or sold (-)	sold at market price in €	additional share premium from sell-ing the shares
March 1	5,000	7	-
June 1	-1,000	10	3,000
Sept 1	-2,000	9	4,000
Dec 1	-1,000	5	-2,000

- The measurement of the treasury shares owned by the company is *at cost*, so the remaining number of treasury shares is 1,000 valued at €7 each.
- The overall additional share premium from selling the stock to the market is 5,000. This is not a profit, but it makes the company wealthier and it shows in equity.

7 Other reporting elements

7.1 Hedge Accounting (IFRS 9)

Hedge accounting is defined as recognition of gains and losses on the hedging instrument in the same period as the recognition of gains and losses on the underlying hedged asset or liability (or firm commitment). For hedge accounting to apply, the forecasted transaction must be probable (likely to occur), the hedge must be highly effective in offsetting fluctuations in the cash flow associated with the foreign currency risk, and the hedging relationship must be properly documented.

The hedge accounting requirements in IFRS 9 are optional. If certain eligibility and qualification criteria are met, hedge accounting allows an entity to reflect risk management activities in the financial statements by matching gains or losses on financial hedging instruments with losses or gains on the risk exposures they hedge.

Qualifying criteria for hedge accounting

A hedging relationship qualifies for hedge accounting only if all of the following criteria are met:

(1) the hedging relationship consists only of eligible hedging instruments and eligible hedged items.

(2) at the inception of the hedging relationship there is formal designation and documentation of the hedging relationship and the entity's risk management objective and strategy for undertaking the hedge.

(3) the hedging relationship meets all of the hedge effectiveness requirements

Example 7-1: Identifying the hedge

Muck AG has sold product to a customer in the USA for an invoiced amount of 20 million USD. The invoice is due to be paid in full in nine months. Muck AG is afraid that due to changes in the foreign currency exchange rate it might receive less EUR in 9 months after receiving the USD and selling these to its bank for EUR. Therefore it enters into a forward contract with the bank to sell 20 million USD 9 months forward at a fixed rate.

In the context of IFRS 9...	
hedged risk	is the foreign currency risk – the risk of movements in the exchange rate
hedged item	is the receivable in foreign currency (an asset in the balance sheet!)
hedging instrument	is the forward contract to sell USD at a fixed rate at a fixed date.

- *Fair value hedge* is a hedge against an asset with a fixed value that changes with the market (supply and demand). For example, an investor may choose to purchase a hedge against changes in the value of a stock. This would be a fixed-value hedge, provided that the stock does not distribute regular cash flow in the form of dividends to shareholders. So how is a fair value hedge recognized? The first step is to determine the fair value of both the hedged item and hedging instrument (derivatives) at the reporting date. Then, any change in fair value (gain or loss) on the hedging instrument in profit or loss is recognized. Finally, the hedging gain or loss on the hedged item in its carrying amount is recognized. If the hedge is completely effective, earnings will not be affected because the gain or loss on the hedged item will offset the gain or loss on the hedging instrument.

- *Cash flow hedge* is a hedge of the exposure to variability in cash flows from financial products. For example, the hedge may be linked to the cash flows generated by an interest-paying bond. If the interest rates shift, affecting the size of the cash flow, then the value of the bond shifts. Cash flow hedges protect against such shifts. To account for cash flow hedges, first the gain or loss on the hedging instrument (derivative) and hedge item at the reporting date is determined. Next, the effective and ineffective portions of the gain or loss on the derivative are calculated. Next, the effective portion of the gain or loss on the derivative in other comprehensive income (OCI) is recognized. This will be called "cash flow hedge reserve" in OCI. Finally, the ineffective portion of the gain or loss on the hedging instrument in profit or loss is recognized.

- *Hedge of a Net Investment in a Foreign Operation* is similar to a cash flow hedge but is used to hedge future changes in currency exposure of a net investment held in another country. For derivatives that qualify as net investment hedges in foreign operations, the effective portions of the change in fair value of the derivatives are recorded in accumulated other comprehensive (loss) income as part of the cumulative translation adjustment. Any ineffective portions of net investment hedges are recognized in other, net expense during the period of change. As with cash flow hedges, even if no actual "cash" transaction takes place then there still could be gains/losses and assets/liabilities that would need to be recognized.

Example 7-2: Cash flow hedge

Muck AG is a producer of aluminum alloy. In t=0, Muck enters into a put option to hedge sales that are expected to happen in t=2 (270 days). The relevant data for the put option is as follows:

Underlying	Aluminum alloy
Contract size	1,000 tons
Spot rate S_0	50€
Exercise price X	50€
Expiration	t=2
Option price	C_0 = 2€ per ton
Intrinsic value	$(X - S) = 50 - 50 = 0$
Time value	$2 - 0 = 2€$

Accounting treatment (journal entry) in t=0

The purchase of the option is recorded with the following journal entry:

Debit record	Credit record
Option (asset) 2,000€	Cash 2,000€

In t=1 (90 days), the following data applies:

Spot rate S_1	46€
Option price	5€ (per ton)
Intrinsic value	$(X - S) = 50 - 46 = 4€$
Time value	$5 - 4 = 1€$

The fair value of the put position has increased from 2,000€ to 5,000€. The option price consists of intrinsic value and time value, so it follows that

Option price = Intrinsic value + Time value

Let's look at the changes of both components of the option price separately:

Put, X=50	t=0	t=1	Change +/–
Option price S	2	5	+3
Intrinsic value X – S	50 – 50 = 0	50 – 46 = 4	+4
Time value	2 – 0 = 2	5 – 4 = 1	– 1

We see that the option price increased by 3€, which is because the intrinsic value of the option increased by 4, whereas the time value decreased by 1. This move in values is recognized in OCI, where the increase in intrinsic value (4) is credited, and the decrease in time value is debited to the OCI. The net effect in the OCI is 3,000 – which is exactly the change in the fair value of the hedging instrument.

Accounting treatment (journal entry) in t=1

The increase in fair value of the option is therefore recognized in t=1 as:

Debit record	Credit record
Option (asset) 3,000€ OCI Option time value reserve 1,000	OCI Cash flow hedge reserve 4,000€

In t=2 (270 days) – at expiration – the following data applies:

Spot rate S_2	40€
Option price	10€ per ton
Intrinsic value	$(X – S) = 50 – 40 = 10€$
Time value	10 – 10 = 0
Sales revenue	1,000 tons × 40€ = 40,000

Again, let's look at the changes of both components of the option price separately:

Put, X=50	t=1	t=2	Change +/−
Option price S	5	10	+5
Intrinsic value X − S	4	50 − 40 = 10	+6
Time value	1	10 − 10 = 0	− 1

Accounting treatment (journal entry) in t=2

The 1,000 tons are sold at the current spot rate and the transaction is recognized as Sales revenue:

Debit record	Credit record
Trade receivable 40,000€	Sales revenue 40,000€

The increase in fair value of the option is therefore recognized in t=1 as:

Debit record	Credit record
Option (asset) 5,000€ OCI Option time value reserve 1,000	OCI Cash flow hedge reserve 6,000€

Note that from the date of purchase until expiration the option has increased in value by 8,000. So the company actually has a net gain of 8,000 coming from the option. With the expiration of the option, the OCI reserves are reclassified, so that the net effect of the hedge – which is 8,000 – is shown in P/L:

Debit record	Credit record
OCI Cash flow hedge reserve 10,000€ Sales 2,000€	Sales 10,000€ OCI Option time value reserve 2,000€

The cash settlement of the option is recorded as:

Debit record	Credit record
Cash 10,000€	Option (asset) 10,000€

In total, Muck AG has realized a sales revenue of 40,000€ in t=2. The spot price for the aluminum has decreased from t=0 to t=2. Without hedging, Muck would have lost revenue. At expiration, the put option has a value of 10,000, which we assume is settled in cash. The option premium Muck paid in t=0 was 2,000€, so that Muck has realized a total profit on the option of 8,000. Hence, Muck's total revenue is 48,000€.

Example 7-3: Fair value hedge

Muck AG is a company engaged in commodities trading. The company recently obtained €5 million short-term borrowing which is secured by the company's inventory of 1,000 tons of copper which it purchased at a cost of €5.2 million. The bank has obligated Muck AG to provide additional collateral in event the value of copper inventories fall below €5 million. On 1 January 2015 (t=0), Muck AG sold the inventories forward by entering into a 12-month futures contract at price of €5,200 per ton. On 30 June 2015 (t=1), i.e. the financial year end of Muck AG, price of copper fell to €4,900 per ton.

- The *hedged instrument* is the instrument whose fair value is shielded using the hedging strategy. In this case, it is the *copper inventory* held by Muck AG.

- *Hedging instrument* on the other hand is the derivative instrument which mitigates the fair value changes of hedged instrument by reversely mimicking its fair value movement.

On 30 June 2015, the fair value of copper inventories held for trading shall be adjusted. The fair value of the copper dropped by 300€ per ton. At the same time, the futures contract has increased in value by 300€ per ton:

Debit record	Credit record
P/L 300,000€	Inventories 300,000€
Derivative (asset) 300,000€	P/L 300,000€

The loss on inventories shall be offset by corresponding gain on the forward transaction. Since the forward transaction entitles Muck AG to sell copper at 5,200€ per ton even though the market price is 4,900€ per ton, it represents a 300€ gain per ton, which translates into 300,000€ gain on 1,000 tons.

7.2 Accounting errors and changes (IAS 8)

Correction of Errors

Material prior period errors should be corrected retrospectively in the financial statements issued after the error is realized. Comparative information should be restated for the prior periods in which the error existed or the beginning balances of assets, liabilities, and equity should be restated for the earliest prior period presented.

Changes in Accounting Policy

A change in accounting policy should be treated retrospectively by restating all prior periods presented and adjusting opening retained earnings (benchmark). If the adjustments relating to prior periods cannot be reasonably determined, the change may be accounted for prospectively. An allowed alternative for the adjustment arising from a retrospective change in accounting policy is to include it in the determination of the net profit or loss for the current period.

A change in accounting policy should be made only if required by statute or by an accounting standard-setting body, or if the change results in a more appropriate presentation of financial statements.

Changes in Accounting Estimate

Changes of accounting estimates should be recognized prospectively in either the current period or current/future period profit or loss depending on the period the change affects. If the change in estimate affects assets, liabilities, or equity, their carrying amount should be adjusted in the period of the change. IFRS account for a change in the depreciation method for existing assets as a change in accounting estimate.

7.3 Disclosures and Segment Reporting (IFRS 8)

With the issuance of IFRS 8 Operating Segments, the new guidance becomes effective for years beginning on or after January 1, 2009.

Operating segments

An operating segment is a component of an entity:

- That engages in business activities from which it may earn revenues and incur expenses
- Whose operating results are regularly reviewed by the entity's *chief operating decision maker* ("CODM") to make decisions about resources to be allocated to the segment and assess its performance.
- For which discrete financial information is available.

Quantitative thresholds

- Information is required to be disclosed separately about an operating segment that meets any of the following quantitative thresholds:

  - Its reported revenue, including both sales to external customers and intersegment sales or transfers, is 10 percent or more of the combined revenue, internal and external, of all operating segments

  - The absolute amount of its reported profit or loss is 10 percent or more of the greater, in absolute amount, of:

- The combined reported profit of all operating segments that did not report a loss; and
- The combined reported loss of all operating segments that reported a loss.

  - Its assets are 10 percent or more of the combined assets of all operating segments.

- If the total external revenue reported by operating segments constitutes less than 75% of the total revenue, additional operating segments shall be identified as reportable segments until at least 75% of the entity's revenue is included in reportable segments.

Reportable segments

IAS 14 required companies to disclose segment information by business (products or services) and by geographic location (of operations or customers). Management of the company had to determine which of the two options should be presented as the primary format based on the risks and returns of the firm's operations. Less disclosure is required for the secondary format. US GAAP, on the other hand, uses the "management approach" whereby segments are determined based on how information is presented to the chief decision maker for allocation of resources. Information regarding product revenue, as well as revenue and assets by geographic location, is required regardless of whether it is used by management to make decisions. IFRS 8 converges international accounting with US GAAP by utilizing the management approach to determine reportable segments. It also requires disclosure of revenue by product and location as well as assets by location.

IFRS 8 allows firms with matrix organization to use whichever criteria results in the most useful information for the financial statement users. Both IFRS 8 and IAS 14 (for the primary segment) require disclosure of segment liabilities.

Disclosure

- An entity shall report a measure of profit or loss and total assets for each reportable segment – only if this information is regularly provided to the CODM.

- Other disclosures are required regarding each reportable segment if specific amounts are reported to the CODM.

- Judgments made by management for the purposes of aggregation of operating segments
  - Description of the operating segments that have been aggregated;
  - Economic indicators considered in determining that segments share similar economic characteristics.
- Operating segment information disclosed is not necessarily IFRS compliant information, as it is based on amounts reported internally.
- Operating segment information disclosed must be reconciled back to IFRS amounts disclosed in the financial statements.
- An entity reports the following geographical information if available:
  - Revenues from external customers both attributed to the entity's country of domicile and attributed to all foreign countries.
  - Non-current assets (except financial instruments, deferred tax assets, post-employment benefit assets and rights arising under insurance contracts) located both in the entity's country of domicile and in foreign countries.
  - The amounts reported are based on the financial information that is used to produce the entity's financial statements.
- An entity provides information about the extent of its reliance on its major customers. If revenues from transactions with a single external customer amount to 10% or more of an entity's revenues, the entity discloses that fact.

7.4 Consolidated Financial Statements (IFRS 10) and Interest in other Entities (IFRS 12)

7.4.1 Background and historical context

There are different motives why entities may acquire "control" of other entities. In this case we call the companies being under "control" by one parent company a "group" – and that includes the parent of course. The combination of these entities can produce advantages such as economies of scale, elimination of competition, spreading of risk across various product lines, access to distribution networks and production techniques and possibly tax benefits.

Users of the financial statements will only be able to make informed economic decisions about the "group" if they have access to a set of financial statements that *combines* the results, assets and liabilities of all the entities within the group.

It was already explained in section 3.7 on page 53 that in the parent's individual financial statements, the investment in the subsidiary is shown at *cost*. This means that in the balance sheet there is just an item "Financial investment" from which the user cannot see what is actually behind this investment – after all the item "Financial investment" stands for a company with a structure, assets, an organization and sales revenues of its own.

As the parent *controls* the subsidiary, from an economic standpoint they are acting as *one* single unit, though from a legal standpoint they are *two* entities. So the parent's financial statements do not present a complete picture of the whole group's economic activities or financial position.

IFRS 10 requires a parent to prepare and present consolidated financial statements when it controls one or more other entities. Consolidated financial statements provide a better reflection of the economic substance of the group whilst preventing manipulation of results through intercompany transactions. The consolidated financial statements also provide a better measurement of the management performance of the entire group.

Preparing consolidated statements starts with the process of selecting which entities are to be included in the consolidated statements and which are not. Normally a majority percentage ownership is indicative of control and/or influence. But it can be achieved by alternative means as well. And that makes this not trivial at all – on the contrary it is of utmost importance – and that is what IFRS 10 is mostly about.

Evaluating if one entity controls another (in other words, when a parent-subsidiary relationship exists) is essential to the preparation of financial statements in accordance with IFRS. The control assessment determines which entities are consolidated in a parent's financial statements and therefore affects a group's reported results, cash flows and financial position – and the activities that are included or not included in the group's balance sheet. Especially when it comes to financial debt – excluding a subsidiary full of debt from the consolidated statements distorts the groups presentation.

As early as 1989, IAS 27 "Consolidated and Separate Financial Statements" was issued. The purpose of IAS 27 was to enhance the relevance, reliability, and comparability of the information contained in consolidated financial statements that a parent prepared for the group of entities it controlled.

Over the years, the inherent flaw in IAS 27 became more and more evident. This flaw was the notion of *control*. IAS 27 required the consolidation of entities that were *controlled* by a reporting entity. To meet this objective, paragraph 4 of IAS 27 defined control as

> *"the power to govern the financial and operating policies of an entity so as to obtain benefits from its activities."*

During the 1990s, this definition was manageable. However, when companies such as Enron began to make use of so-called special purpose entities, the notion of control was exposed to some degree of manipulation.

Accordingly, in 1998, the SIC (the Standards Interpretation Committee) of the International Accounting Standards Committee released Issue No. 12 (SIC 12) focusing on the requirements of IAS 27 within the context of special purpose entities. The problem was that SIC 12 placed emphasis on *risks and rewards* in the analysis of assessing control, an approach that was not quite the same as the definition of control in IAS 27. The result was inconsistent application of the concept of control, intensified by a lack of clear guidance as to how to determine which entities were within the scope of IAS 27 and which were within the scope of SIC 12.

Why did this matter? Instead of focusing on "substance," the assessment of control relied on "form." Specifically, the assessment of "whether an investor had a majority of the risks and rewards" became the defining question. The consequence of this was that entities had an incentive to structure opportunities to achieve particular accounting outcomes – e.g. hide debt in subsidiaries, which did not show in the consolidated statements, as per definition the criteria for consolidation were not met.

In 2011 the IASB issued two new standards that deal with consolidated statements and accompanying disclosures—IFRS 10, "Consolidated Financial Statements" and IFRS 12, "Disclosure of Interests in Other Entities." The new requirements will be effective beginning in 2013. The standards employ a new singular definition of control that focuses on the power to direct the activities of an entity, exposure to variable returns, and a linkage between power and returns.

Unlike the FASB, which currently has separate control models for voting interest versus variable interest entities, IFRS 10 provides a single model for assessing whether an investor controls an investee and provides more extensive guidance on applying this model. IFRS 10 applies to all investees and replaces the previous models for determining control found in IAS 27 and the interpretive guidance for special purpose entities found in SIC-12. It replaces the corresponding requirements of both IAS 27 "Consolidated and Separate Financial Statements" (IAS 27) and SIC-12 "Consolidation – Special Purpose Entities" (SIC-12). Although SIC-12 is an interpretation of IAS 27, some commentators believe that it established a somewhat different model for assessing control over special purpose entities.

7.4.2   Control model under IFRS 10

The basis for the single consolidation model of IFRS 10 rests on assessing whether a reporting entity has control of another entity regardless of its nature. Paragraph 6 stipulates that an investor controls an investee when it is exposed, or has rights to variable returns from its involvement with the investee and has the ability to affect those returns through its power over the investee.

So the control model under IFRS 10 is based on the existence of three elements of control. When all of these three elements of control are present then an investor is considered to control an investee and consolidation is required. When one or more of the elements is not present, an investor will not consolidate but instead be required to determine the nature of its relationship with the investee (e.g. significant influence, joint control) and the appropriate accounting under the requisite IFRS.

The three elements of control which are the basis for consolidation under IFRS 10 are show in Table 7-1:

Table 7-1: Elements of control IFRS 10

Power over the investee	Exposure or rights to variable returns[2]	Ability to use power to affect returns[3]
Existing rights that give the current ability to direct *relevant activities*[1] of the investee, specifically the activities that significantly affect the investee's returns.	Returns are not fixed and have the potential to *vary* with the performance of the investee.	There must be link between power and returns.

[1] Relevant activities include

- Selling and purchasing of goods or services
- Managing financial assets during their life
- Selecting, acquiring or disposing of assets
- Researching/developing new products or processes
- Determining a funding structure or obtaining funding.

Decisions on relevant activities include:
- Establishing operating and capital decisions & budgets
- Appointing, remunerating, and terminating an investee's key management personnel (KMP) or service providers.

[2] Variable returns include

- Dividends, interest from debt securities issued by the investee, changes in the value of the investor's investment in that investee
- Fees from servicing assets or liabilities, fees and exposure to loss from providing credit or liquidity support, residual interests in net assets on liquidation, tax benefits, and access to future liquidity
- Returns unavailable to other interest holders (like synergies or cost savings).

[3] Ability to use power

- A parent must not only have power over an investee and exposure or rights to variable returns from its involvement with the investee, a parent must also have the ability to use its power over the investee to affect its returns from its involvement with the investee.
- When assessing whether an investor controls an investee an investor with decision-making rights determines whether it acts as principal or as an agent of other parties.
- A number of factors are considered in making this assessment. For instance, the remuneration of the decision-maker is considered in determining whether it is an agent. An investor that is an agent does not control an investee when it exercises decision-making rights delegated to it.

7.4.3 Exemptions from preparing consolidated financial statements

A parent need not present consolidated financial statements if it meets all of the following conditions:

- it is a wholly-owned subsidiary or is a partially-owned subsidiary of another entity and its other owners, including those not otherwise entitled to vote, have been informed about, and do not object to, the parent not presenting consolidated financial statements
- its debt or equity instruments are not traded in a public market (a domestic or foreign stock exchange or an over-the-counter market, including local and regional markets)
- it did not file, nor is it in the process of filing, its financial statements with a securities commission or other regulatory organization for the purpose of issuing any class of instruments in a public market, and
- its ultimate or any intermediate parent of the parent produces consolidated financial statements available for public use that comply with IFRS.
- post-employment benefit plans or other long-term employee benefit plans to which IAS 19 Employee Benefits applies are not required to apply the requirements of IFRS 10.

7.4.4 Special Purpose Entities (SPE) and structured entities

The term Special Purpose Entities (SPE) is used to describe entities that would be considered to be within the scope of SIC-12. SIC-12 describes SPEs only in general terms, so deciding whether a particular entity is an SPE can require judgement. IFRS 10 does not refer to SPEs, but instead refers to entities that have been designed so that voting or similar rights are not the dominant factor in assessing control. These are described as "structured entities" (in IFRS 12 "Disclosure of Interests in Other Entities"). IFRS 10 includes application guidance for assessing control over such entities. In practice we expect that most (but not all) entities previously regarded as SPE under SIC-12 would be structured entities under IFRS 10.

7.4.5 Types of combinations

Table 7-2: Types of business combinations

Type	Acquiring company A	Acquired company B
Statutory merger through asset acquisition Concept $A + B = A$	Asset purchase: A acquires assets and often liabilities of B	Dissolves and becomes defunct (goes out of business). As part of the merger process, the shareholders of B receive - payment for their shares and/or - shares in corporation A

Statutory merger through capital stock acquisition Concept *A + B = A*	Stock purchase: A acquires all stock of B, then transfers assets and liabilities to its own book	Dissolves as a separate corporation, or remaining as a division of the acquiring company As part of the merger process, the shareholders of B receive - payment for their shares and/or - shares in corporation A
Statutory consolidation through capital stock or asset acquisition Concept *A + B = C*	Newly created to receive assets or capital stock of original companies	Original companies may dissolve while remaining as separate divisions of newly created company
Acquisition of more than 50 percent of the voting rights	Acquires stock that is recognized as a "Financial Investment"; controls decision making of acquired company	Remains in existence as legal corporation, though now a subsidiary of A.

Acquisition as an Asset Purchase or a Stock Purchase

Acquisition – Acquired company dissolved	
Asset Purchase	*Stock Purchase*
Company A obtains *the assets, and often the liabilities, of company B* in exchange for cash, other assets, liabilities, stock, or a combination of these. Company B normally dissolves itself as a legal corporation. Thus, only the acquiring company remains in existence, having absorbed the acquired net assets directly into its own operations.	Company A obtains *all of the capital stock of company B* in exchange for cash, other assets, liabilities, stock, or a combination of these. This statutory merger is achieved by obtaining equity securities rather than by buying the target company's assets. The purchase of a sufficient number of voting shares of a corporation's stock, enabling the acquiring corporation to exercise control over the target corporation is often facilitated by a tender offer to the target corporation's shareholders. The tender offer is publicly advertised, available to all shareholders, and offers to pay a higher-than-market price (premium) for shares of the target corporation. All of the capital stock of a company can be acquired with the assets and liabilities then transferred to the buyer followed by the seller's dissolution. Because stock is obtained, the acquiring company must gain 100 percent control of all shares before legally dissolving the subsidiary.

Acquisition with the acquired company not dissolved
One company achieves legal control over another by acquiring a majority of voting stock. Although control is present, no dissolution takes place; each company remains in existence as an incorporated operation.
Separate incorporation is frequently preferred because of a better utilization of such factors as licenses, trade names, employee loyalty, and the company's reputation when the subsidiary maintains its own legal identity. Moreover, maintaining an independent information system for a subsidiary often enhances its market value for an eventual sale or initial public offering as a stand-alone entity.
Because *the asset and liability account balances are not physically combined* as in statutory mergers and consolidations, each company continues to maintain an independent accounting system. To reflect the combination, the acquiring company enters the takeover transaction into its own records by establishing a single investment asset account. However, the newly acquired subsidiary omits any recording of this event; its stock is simply transferred to the parent from the subsidiary's shareholders. Thus, the subsidiary's financial records are not directly affected by a takeover.

7.4.6 Types of investments from a reporting perspective

The table below provides an overview of the different classifications of investments and the accounting treatment required.

Control/Influence	Indicative shareholding	Classification	Accounting treatment
Control	> 50 percent	Subsidiary	Full consolidation (Acquisition Method)
Joint control	50/50	Joint venture	Equity Method
Significant influence	20-50 percent	Associate	Equity Method
Insignificant influence	< 20 percent	Trade investment	Financial Instrument

7.4.7 Acquisition Method

Recognition of an acquisition

Generally, a business combination must be accounted for by applying the **acquisition method**, which requires assets acquired and liabilities assumed to be measured at their fair values at the acquisition date. This comprises the following four steps:

(1) Identification of acquirer

(2) Determine the date at which the acquirer obtains control

    (3) Recognition and measurement of the identifiable assets acquired, the liabilities assumed and any *non-controlling interest* (NCI, formerly called minority interest) in the acquiree

    (4) Recognition and measurement of goodwill or a gain from a bargain purchase.

Acquisition Method

The acquisition method replaced the purchase method. For combinations resulting in complete ownership, it is distinguished by four characteristics.

    (1) All assets acquired and liabilities assumed in the combination are recognized and measured at their individual fair values (with few exceptions).

    (2) The fair value of the consideration transferred provides a starting point for valuing and recording a business combination.

        a. The consideration transferred includes cash, securities, and contingent performance obligations.

        b. Direct combination costs are expensed as incurred.

        c. Stock issuance costs are recorded as a reduction in paid-in capital.

        d. The fair value of any non-controlling interest also adds to the valuation of the acquired firm.

    (3) Any excess of the fair value of the consideration transferred over the net amount assigned to the individual assets acquired and liabilities assumed is recognized by the acquirer as goodwill.

    (4) Any excess of the net amount assigned to the individual assets acquired and liabilities assumed over the fair value of the consideration transferred is recognized by the acquirer as a "gain on bargain purchase."

In-process research and development acquired in a business combination is recognized as an asset at its acquisition-date fair value.

Goodwill as an asset

In real life we would not expect that the purchase price for the acquiree is identical to its net worth (which means its net assets = assets minus liabilities, or equity). Usually, the owners of a profitable business will expect to receive *more* in exchange for the company than its net asset value.

This additional amount arises for various reasons. It is quite likely that the assets recognized in the statement of financial position do not represent *all* the assets of the firm.

- For example, intangibles such as good reputation, the existing organization of the company, its market share, its competent employees and customer loyalty might be very valuable to a buyer - but none of these appear in a balance sheet. So there may be good reasons to pay a price much higher than the book values of the acquiree.

- On the other hand, it may well happen that buyers want to have the acquiree at any cost – so they will be willing to pay huge premiums and then come up with fancy arguments why the acquisition is such a good idea. These agency problem–induced motives result in that managers gain from mergers and acquisitions, rather than shareholders.[5]

  - According to the *managerialism theory of mergers*, poorly monitored managers will pursue mergers to maximize their corporation's asset size because managerial compensation is usually based on firm size.

  - The *free cash theory of mergers* states that managers will use free cash flow to invest in mergers that have negative net present values in order to build corporate empires from which the managers will derive personal benefits, including greater compensation.

  - The *managerial entrenchment theory of mergers* holds that unmonitored managers will try to build corporate empires through the pursuit of negative NPV mergers.

  - The *hubris hypothesis of corporate takeovers* states that some managers overestimate their own managerial capabilities and pursue takeovers with the belief that they can better manage their takeover target than the target's current management team can.

So the difference between the cost of investment and the fair value of the net assets acquired is known as *goodwill* on acquisition. The *goodwill* is what the acquirer pays for the company in excess of the net assets that can be seen and identified on a balance sheet. Accounting-wise, the purchase price (the cost) is what the acquirer pays – the equity of the acquiree (the net assets) is what he receives – if the purchase price is higher than the net assets we will have a positive goodwill.

Measurement of goodwill

Goodwill is measured as the difference between the aggregate of

- the value of the consideration transferred (generally at fair value),
- the amount of any non-controlling interest, and

---

[5] There is a lot of research on acquisition motives. These are only two examples: Roll, Richard (1986): The hubris hypothesis of corporate takeovers. In: Journal of business, S. 197–216. Seth, Anju; Song, Kean P.; Pettit, Richardson (2000): Synergy, managerialism or hubris? An empirical examination of motives for foreign acquisitions of US firms. In: Journal of international business studies 31 (3), S. 387–405.

- in a business combination achieved in stages, the acquisition-date fair value of the acquirer's previously-held equity interest in the acquiree, and the net of the acquisition-date amounts of the identifiable assets acquired and the liabilities assumed.

This can be written in simplified equation form as follows:

Goodwill = Consideration transferred (in simpler terms: the purchase price)

+ Amount of non-controlling interests

+ Fair value of previous equity interests

– Net assets recognized

If the difference above is negative, the resulting gain is a bargain purchase in profit or loss, which may arise in circumstances such as a forced seller acting under compulsion. However, before any bargain purchase gain is recognized in profit or loss, the acquirer is required to undertake a review to ensure the identification of assets and liabilities is complete, and that measurements appropriately reflect consideration of all available information.

Example 7-4 Goodwill

On August 1, 2013 Muck AG paid 800,000€ cash for all of the issued and outstanding common stock of Auzzi Corp. The carrying values for Auzzi's assets and liabilities on August 1 on its balance sheet are:

Statement of Financial Position Auzzi SA as of August 1, 2013			
Assets		Liabilities & Equity	
Cash	150,000€	Liabilities	130,000€
Accounts receivable	180,000€		
Capitalized software costs	320,000€	Equity	620,000€
Goodwill	100,000€		
Total	750,000€	Total	750,000€

On August 1, Auzzi's accounts receivable had a fair value of $140,000. Additionally, Auzzi's research and development was estimated to have a fair value of $200,000. All other items were stated at their fair values. On Muck's August 1 consolidated balance sheet, how much is reported for goodwill?

To determine goodwill, we need a new revalued balance sheet – now with fair values, and not any more with the carrying values from accounting. And we will only include so-called **identifiable** assets. Unlike other assets, **we consider goodwill as unidentifiable** because we presume it emerges from several other assets acting together to produce an expectation of enhanced profitability. Goodwill essentially captures all sources of profitability beyond what can be expected from simply summing the fair values of the acquired firm's assets and liabilities. So goodwill is by no means a "normal asset" – if there was anything like that at all. But existing goodwill will no be taken over into Muck's balance sheet, so it does not appear on the revalued balance sheet either.

Note also that the "old" carrying values followed the *going concern* assumption – but now that the company has been acquired, accounting people would feel uncomfortable with the idea to still use "old" accounting values if control has been transferred. So fair values for Auzzi have to be determined – which in real life is a lot of work for accountants and other specialists. With the given information on Auzzi's fair values, we can now prepare the revalued balance sheet:

Statement of Financial Position (fair values) Auzzi SA as of August 1, 2013			
Assets			*Liabilities & Equity*
Cash	150,000€	Liabilities	130,000€
Accounts receivable	140,000€		
Capitalized software costs	320,000€	Equity	680,000€
Research & Development	200,000€		
Total	810,000€	Total	810,000€

So Auzzi's identifiable assets net of liabilities (net assets or equity) is 680,000€. But Muck paid 800,000€ for the company, so Muck paid 120,000€ in excess of values that can be seen in the balance sheet. These 120,000€ are Goodwill to be recognized in Muck's balance sheet.

7.4.8   Consolidation of balance sheet items

All assets and liabilities of the parent and subsidiaries are added together line by line, with items appearing as assets in one company and liabilities or equity in another being cancelled out ("consolidated").

- The main items which are cancelled out include intra-company balances, and the parent's investment in the subsidiary with its portion of the subsidiary's equity acquired.
- These cancellations only take place in the group accounts. The individual company accounts of the parent and the subsidiary are not affected.

Intra-company balances can arise for a number of reasons, for example:

- loans issued between group companies;
- intra-company sales, where the goods are transferred between group companies;
- current accounts which record the movement of goods, services or money between group companies.

- All intra-company balances are eliminated on consolidation. If the balances do not agree at the year-end, this will normally be due to either inventory or cash in transit. These in-transit items are shown as assets in the consolidated Statement of Financial Position and the corresponding intra-company balances cancelled out.

Partly owned subsidiaries

- If the parent company does not own 100% of the subsidiary's shares, the remainder of the shares are held by other shareholders, known as 'non-controlling interests'.
- In this case, the Consolidated Statement of Financial Position will still include all of the subsidiary's assets and liabilities (*"full consolidation"*), as the parent controls them all. However, an amount representing the net assets attributable to the 'non-controlling interests' will also be separately disclosed on the face of the Consolidated Statement of Financial Position.

Consolidation of Income and expenses

The income and expenses of a parent and its subsidiaries are added together line by line, i.e. consolidated. Items appearing as income in one group company and expenditure in another are cancelled out. The main items which are cancelled out include:

- intra-company sales/purchases
- intra-group charges such as management charges, interest on loans, rent, etc.
- Note that these cancellations take place only in the group accounts. The individual company accounts for the parent and the subsidiary are not affected.

Consolidation of cash flows

The preparation of a single-entity statement of cash flows as set out in IAS 7 Statement of Cash Flows is dealt with in section 3.8 on page 54. A Consolidated Statement of Cash Flows will not include cash flows within the group, as it is assumed that all the companies within the group are in effect acting as a single unit.

7.4.9   Accounting for Associates: the Equity Method

Significant influence

The equity method is applied to recognize the investment in a so-called "associate". An associate is an entity (including an unincorporated entity such as a partnership) over which the investor has (only) "significant influence" (and no "control") and that is, neither a subsidiary, nor an interest in a joint venture.

Significant influence is the power to participate in the financial and operating policy decisions of the investee but is not control or joint control over those policies. Significant influence is presumed to exist where an investor holds, directly or indirectly (e.g. through subsidiaries), 20% or more of the voting power of the investee, unless it can be clearly demonstrated that this is not the case. Significant influence is presumed not to exist where an investor holds, directly or indirectly less than 20% of the voting power of the investee, unless such influence can be clearly demonstrated. A substantial or majority ownership by another investor does not necessarily preclude an investor from having significant influence.

Indications of significant influence are:

- representation on the board of directors (or equivalent governing body);
- participation in policy-making processes;
- material transactions between the investor and the investee;
- interchange of management personnel; or
- provision of essential technical information.

Recognizing the investment in an associate

The associate's assets and liabilities are not consolidated with the investor's (i.e. not added together), as the investor does not have control. Instead, the investment in the associate is disclosed separately within non-current assets.

The investor reports its share of the associate's net income in his own income statement as an income (which will technically increase equity on the right side of the balance sheet), and at the same time it increases the "Investment in associates" asset on the left side of the balance sheet by the same amount.

For any dividends paid to the investor, the "Investment in associates" asset will decrease (as this is the part of the asset value that has actually been received as cash) and consequently the cash position in the balance sheet will increase.

Example 7-5: Equity Method

Muck Company acquires 25 percent of the voting stock of Dillon Corporation for 4,000,000€ on January 1, 2014. During 2014, Dillon reported net income of 1,500,000€ and paid dividends of 200,000€. Both companies have December 31 year-ends.

Assumption 1: Dillon's carrying value at acquisition was 16,000,000€

Acquiring the 25 percent share and paying for it is recognized at cost:

Debit record	Credit record
Investment in associates 4,000,000€	Cash 4,000,000€

At the end of 2014, the increase in value for the investor is taken from the net income of the associate. Dillon's net income is 1,500,000€, so Muck's share is 375,000, which increases the carrying value of the investment, and at the same time is income in Muck's income statement:

Debit record	Credit record
Investment in associates 375,000€	Equity in Associates earnings 375,000€

The dividends received (50,000€) will be deducted from the investment account:

Debit record	Credit record
Cash 50,000€	Investment in associates 50,000€

At the end of 2014, Muck's Investment in Associates account has a carrying value of 4,325,000€.

Assumption 2: Dillon's carrying value at acquisition was 10,000,000€; goodwill to be amortized over 10 years

Acquiring the 25 percent share and paying for it is recognized at cost:

Debit record	Credit record
Investment in associates 4,000,000€	Cash 4,000,000€

Muck bought the 25% share for 4,000,000€, but this share has a carrying value of "only" 2,500,000€, which leads to a Goodwill of 1,500,000€. The annual amortization will therefore be 150,000€.

Again, at the end of 2014, the increase in value for the investor is taken from the share in net income of the associate (375,000) minus the amortization of 150,000. The journal entry is therefore:

Debit record	Credit record
Investment in associates 225,000€	Equity in Associates earnings 225,000€

The dividends received (50,000€) will be deducted from the investment account:

Debit record	Credit record
Cash 50,000€	Investment in associates 50,000€

At the end of 2014, Muck's Investment in Associates account has therefore a carrying value of 4,175,000€.

8 Mathematical appendix

8.1 Review: Time Value of Money

8.1.1 Simple and compound interest

Interest on money invested can be calculated in two ways – as *simple interest* or as *compound interest*. Simple interest is earned only on the principal amout invested – whereas compound interest is earned on both the principal and on previously accumulated interest.

Discrete compounding means that interest is earned periodically and accrued to the account in regular time intervals – we assume here the interest accrues at the end of a compounding period. In an illustrative way of description, compounding can be viewed as a growth process. An amount of money grows over time – the question remains, exactly when is the growth happening? In discrete compounding, the growth happens *stepwise*, e.g. at the end of a year, at the end of every 6 months, or at the end of each month etc.[6]

- For discrete compounding we usually start with a nominal interest rate per year. If the compounding period is exactly one year, then the m=1.
- If there are two sub-periods per year, then the interest conversion period m is 2. In this case, compounding happens at the end of the first six months, then again at the end of the year.
- For m=4 we compound at the end of each quarter, and so forth.

Continuous compounding is a theoretical construct as it assumes an infinite number of compounding periods per year, with sub-periods to have a length of nearly zero. Consequently, interest payments are accrued continuously. Continuous compounding is an exponential process modelled with the e-function.

---

[6] The accrual of interest could be contracted and calculated for any point in time, but in most financial applications we assume that the compounding happens at the end of a period.

Table 8-1: Overview of interest calculation formulae

Present Value PV_0, Future Value at the end of n-th year FV_n nominal interest rate i_{nom}, years n, compounding periods within a year m		
Simple interest	Compound interest	
	Discrete compounding	Continuous compounding
$FV_n = PV_0 + (n \times i_{nom} \times PV_0)$ $FV_n = PV_0(1 + ni_{nom})$	$FV_n = PV_0 \times \left(1 + \dfrac{i_{nom}}{m}\right)^{m \times n}$	$FV_n = PV_0 \times e^{i_{nom} \times n}$

For each formula in the table, if all but one variable are known, we can simply solve the equation for the unknown variable and determine the missing value.

For the two compound interest scenarios, the *annualized* growth rate – which is the percentage growth rate per year – from PV_0 to FV_n is the **effective annual interest rate i_{eff}**:

$$i_{eff} = \sqrt[n]{\frac{FV_n}{PV_0}} - 1$$

Example 8-1: Determine a future value

Muck owns 5000€. If Muck puts his money in a bank account and does not spend it, how much will he have after 15 years, assuming the nominal annual interest rate is 4.8% and interest is compounded annually? What is the future value if the interest was compounded monthly?

With annual compounding:

$$FV = PV \cdot (1 + i_{nom})^n = 5{,}000 \times 1{,}048^{15} \approx 10{,}101.58$$

With monthly compounding:

$$FV = PV \cdot \left(1 + \frac{i_{nom}}{m}\right)^{n \times m} = 5{,}000 \times \left(1 + \frac{0.048}{12}\right)^{12 \times 15} \approx 10{,}257.42$$

Example 8-2: Determine a present value

Muck needs 30,000€ in 17 years from now. If interest is compounded four times a year, at a nominal annual interest rate of 2.4 percent, how much will he have to invest in t=0?

$$FV = PV \times \left(1+\frac{r}{m}\right)^{m \times n} \Rightarrow 30,000 = PV \times \left(1+\frac{0,024}{4}\right)^{4 \times 17} \Rightarrow PV \approx 19,973.7€$$

Muck will have to invest 19,973.7€ in t=0 at an annual interest rate of 2.4 percent, which is compounded four times a year, to have 30,000€ in 17 years.

Example 8-3: Determine the number of years for compounding

How long (in years) does it take to increase capital by 50 percent, if interest of 2.7% per year is compounded annually?

To "increase capital by 50 percent" means that the future value is 50 percent higher than the present value – so the relationship between future value and present value can be described as

$$FV = 1.5 \times PV$$

$$\Rightarrow \frac{FV}{PV} = 1.5$$

Then we take the compounding formula and rearrange for n by taking the natural logarithm on both sides of the equation:

$$FV_n = PV_0 \times (1+i)^n$$

$$\Rightarrow \ln\left(\frac{FV_t}{PV_0}\right) = n \times \ln(1+i)$$

$$\Rightarrow t = \frac{\ln\left(\frac{1.5PV}{PV}\right)}{\ln(1+0,027)} = \frac{\ln 1,5}{\ln 1,027} \cong 15.22 \text{ years}$$

Example 8-4: Present Value of an annuity

A statement was posted in the Internet lately:

> "Had you purchased 1 share of Coca-Cola stock in 1919 for $40,
>
> that stock would be worth 9.8 million Dollars today."

Assume that the statement is correct. What would be the average annual return on the stock with annual compounding from end of year 1919 to end of year 2015?

It is 96 years from end of year 1919 until end of year 2015. Present value is 40, future value is 9.8 million, and n=96. We substitute these values in the compounding formula and solve for i:

$$FV = PV \cdot (1+i)^n \Rightarrow 9{,}800{,}000 = 40 \cdot (1+i)^{96}$$

$$\Rightarrow i = \sqrt[96]{\frac{9{,}800{,}000}{40}} - 1 = 0.1379866 \cong 13.8\% \, p.a.$$

For the given data, over a total of 96 years the Coca-Cola stock yielded on average 13.8 percent per year.

8.1.2   Present Value of an Annuity

An annuity is a cash flow consisting of (not necessarily but often) equal amounts to be paid at constant intervals. Examples of annuities are saving plans (with a constant amount and at constant intervals), pension payments, mortgage payments or coupon payments of a bond. The constant intervals may be days, months or years or any other period.

Though payments for each period can be at any time within the period, as the standard case we will assume they are being paid at the end of a period (ordinary annuity). An annuity in which payments are made at the beginning of the period is called an annuity due.

If not stated otherwise, we study annuities under the following assumptions:

(1) The time interval in which payments are made is fixed or constant.

(2) The periodic payments are equal in size.

(3) The payments are made at the end of a period.

(4) The payment period is identical to the interest conversion period.

The coupon payment of a bond is an annuity, as it is a fixed cash flow (the coupon interest) being paid (in most cases) at either the end of a year (annually) or every six months (semi-annually).

The present value of an annuity of is the value today of the total cash flow, discounted with the appropriate interest rate.

The present value annuity factor (PVAF) is the present value of an annuity of exactly 1€ that is being paid at the end of n consecutive years.

$$PVAF(i;n) = \frac{(1+i)^n - 1}{(1+i)^n \cdot i}$$
(8-1)

Example 8-5: Present Value of an annuity

Muck has just purchased a new car on credit. The dealer's installment plan calls for five payments of 8,000€ to be paid at the end of each year of the following five years, starting at the end of the first year. The relevant interest rate is 11 percent.

This is the payment schedule on a timeline:

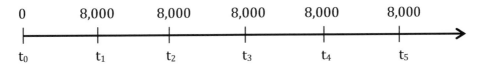

Discounting each payment with the interest rate of 11 percent yields the present value of the annuity:

$$\frac{8,000}{1,11^1} + \frac{8,000}{1,11^2} + \frac{8,000}{1,11^3} + \frac{8,000}{1,11^4} + \frac{8,000}{1,11^5} = 29,567.18$$

The alternative way of determining the annuity is by using the PVA-factor in formula (8-1) for n=5 payments and the annual interest rate of i=0.11:

$$PVAF(i = 0.11; n = 5) = \frac{(1+i)^n - 1}{(1+i)^n \times i} = \frac{(1.11)^5 - 1}{(1.11)^5 \times 0.11} = 3.695897$$

The PVAF of 3.695897 represents the present value – the value today – of exactly 1€ to be paid at the end of each of the next five years for the given interest rate.

Since the payment for Muck is not 1€ each year, but 8.000€, we multiply the PVAF by 8,000 to get the present value of the annuity (PVA):

$$PVA = 3.695897 \times 8,000 = 29,567.18$$

The present value of the annuity is 29,567.18€. If the financing cost is 11 percent, then the result could be interpreted that the car has a cash price of 29,567.18€ – but since Muck is financing it, it cost him in total 5 x 8,000€ = 40,000€. So he will be paying more than 10,000€ in interest to buy the new car.

8.1.3   Future Value of an Annuity

The payment schedule for a five-year annuity C may look like this on a timeline:

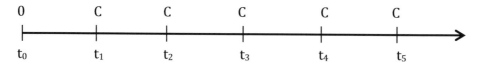

We determined the value in t=0 of an annuity of C=1€ to be the Present Value of an Annuity factor, which only depends on the number of payments n and the applicable interest rate i. If we compound this PVAF to the end of the n-th year, we have the Future Value of the Annuity.

The Future Value of an Annuity-factor (FVAF) is therefore

$$FVAF = PVAF \times (1+i)^n = \frac{(1+i)^n - 1}{(1+i)^n \times i} \times (1+i)^n = \frac{(1+i)^n - 1}{i} \qquad (8\text{-}2)$$

Example 8-6: Future Value of an annuity

Muck decides to save 12,000€ a year for the next four years. He can earn a 6 percent return on these savings. How much will he have at the end of the fourth year?

Step 1: Determine FVAF for n=4 and i=0,06.

$$FVAF\left(4\,yrs;6\%\right) = \frac{(1.06)^4 - 1}{0.06} = 4.374616$$

Step 2: Multiply FVAF with the annuity.

$$FVA = 12{,}000 \times 4.374616 = 52{,}581.27$$

He will save in total 48,000€. Since he also earns some interest on what he saves, his total payoff will be 52.581,27 – the difference being the interest earned, which is 4,581.27€.

Example 8-7: Future Value of an annuity – monthly compounding

---

Muck decides to save 12,000€ a year for the next four years in installments of 12 monthly payments of 1,000€. He can earn a 6 percent interest compounded monthly. How much will he have at the end of the fourth year?

Since i is the nominal interest rate per period and since interest is compounded monthly and the payments are monthly, we have $i = 0.06/12 = 0{,}005$ for $n = 12 \times 4 = 48$ payments of 1,000.

Step 1: Determine FVAF for $n=4\times12=48$ and $i=0,065$.

$$FVAF\left(48;0.005\right)=\frac{\left(1.0005\right)^{48}-1}{0.005}=54.09783222$$

Step 2: Multiply FVAF with the annuity.

$$FVA=1{,}000\times54.09783222=54{,}097.83$$

Like in Example 8-6, he will save in total 48,000€. Since he also earnes some interest on what he saves, his total payoff will be 54.097,83 – the difference being the interest earned, which is 6,097.83€. Comparing this result with the payoff in Example 8-6, we notice the effect of the different cash flow and the different compounding scheme. In this example, Muck saved his money earlier – 1,000 in every month instead of 12,000 at the end of each year. These payments earned the interest earlier – resulting in the difference of 6.097.83€ between this example and Example 8-6.

8.1.4   Converting a Present Value into an Annuity

Instead of transforming an annuity into a present value, we can also convert a present value in an equivalent annuity. To determine the present value of the annuity PVA (unknown variable) we made use of the PVAF and multiplied it with the annuity C (both known values):

$$PVA=C\times\frac{\left(1+i\right)^{n}-1}{\left(1+i\right)^{n}\times i}$$

Now we rearrange the equation and the annuity becomes the unknown variable, and since present value and PVAF are known, the equation changes to:

$$C=PVA\div\frac{\left(1+i\right)^{n}-1}{\left(1+i\right)^{n}\times i}=PVA\times\frac{\left(1+i\right)^{n}\times i}{\left(1+i\right)^{n}-1}$$

Either we divide the present value by the PVAF, or we multiply the present value with the inverse of the PVAF to get the annuity amount.

Example 8-8: Loan contract annuity – annual compounding

Muck Inc. management decides to take a 10-year-loan in the amount of 3,000,000€. What are the annual payments for a nominal annual interest rate of 8 percent? The annuity contains both interest payment and return of the principal.

Step 1: Determine the PVAF for 8 percent and 10 years.

$$PVAF(8\%;10\,yrs.) = \frac{(1+i)^n - 1}{(1+i)^n \times i} = \frac{1.08^{10} - 1}{1.08^{10} \times 0.08} = 6.710081399$$

Step 2: Determine the annuity by dividing the present value (3m€) by the PVAF:

$$C = 3,000,000 \div 6.710081399 = 447,088.47€$$

Step 3: Show the full amortization schedule

End of year n	annuity	interest	repayment of principal	outstanding principal	accumulated interest	accumulated repayment
	A	$B = D \times i$	$C = A - B$	$D_n = D_{n-1} - C$	$E = \sum B$	$F = \sum C$
0	0	0	0	3,000,000.00	0	0
1	447,088.47	240,000.00	207,088.47	2,792,911.53	240,000.00	207,088.47
2	447,088.47	223,432.92	223,655.54	2,569,255.99	463,432.92	430,744.01
3	447,088.47	205,540.48	241,547.99	2,327,708.00	668,973.40	672,292.00
4	447,088.47	186,216.64	260,871.83	2,066,836.18	855,190.04	933,163.82
5	447,088.47	165,346.89	281,741.57	1,785,094.61	1,020,536.94	1,214,905.39
6	447,088.47	142,807.57	304,280.90	1,480,813.71	1,163,344.50	1,519,186.29
7	447,088.47	118,465.10	328,623.37	1,152,190.34	1,281,809.60	1,847,809.66
8	447,088.47	92,175.23	354,913.24	797,277.10	1,373,984.83	2,202,722.90
9	447,088.47	63,782.17	383,306.30	413,970.80	1,437,767.00	2,586,029.20
10	447,088.47	33,117.66	413,970.80	0.00	1,470,884.66	3,000,000.00

A. At the end of each of the ten years, Muck Inc. has to pay 447,088.47€.

B. Interest each year is calculated by multiplying the outstanding principal from the beginning of a period with the interest rate.

C. The payment (the annuity) is constant, but the interest portion declines – which means the repayment of the principal is always the annuity minus the interest portion. Since the interest portion declines each year, the repayment portion of the principal increases each year.

D. The outstanding principal at the end of a period is the outstanding principal from the beginning of the period minus what has been repaid at that period (column C).

E. In total, Muck Inc. pays almost 1,470,885€ only for interest.

F. All of his loan repayments add up to the total loan amount.

Example 8-9: Loan contract annuity – monthly payments

Muck borrows 200,000€ from the bank to purchase a house. The bank charges nominal interest at a rate of 6 percent a year on the unpaid balance. Muck pays monthly installments over 20 years. What is the annuity each month if the loan is to be amortized at the end of the 20 years?

Step 1: Determine the PVAF for 6 percent annually, which is 6%/12 = 0.5% monthly.

The periods are now measured in months, so that 20 x 12 = 240 months:

$$PVAF(0.5\%;240m.) = \frac{\left(1+\dfrac{i_{nom}}{m}\right)^{n\times m}-1}{\left(1+\dfrac{i_{nom}}{m}\right)^{n\times m}\times\dfrac{i_{nom}}{m}} = \frac{1.005^{240}-1}{1.005^{240}\times 0.005} = 139.5807717$$

Step 2: Determine the annuity by dividing the present value of 200,000 by the PVAF:

$$C = 200,000 \div 139.5807717 = 1,432.86€$$

Step 3: Amortization schedule with first and last 10 months, respectively. For ease of reading, all numbers have been rounded without decimals. As we see in the last row of the table, to finance a house with purchasing price 200,000€, the financing cost – the interest – totals almost 144,000€.

End of year n	annuity	interest	repayment of principal	outstanding principal	accumulated interest	accumulated repayment
	A	$B = D \times i$	$C = A - B$	$D_n = D_{n-1} - C$	$E = \sum B$	$F = \sum C$
0	-	-	-	200,000	-	-
1	1,433	1,000	433	199,567	1,000	433
2	1,433	998	435	199,132	1,998	868
3	1,433	996	437	198,695	2,993	1,305
4	1,433	993	439	198,256	3,987	1,744
5	1,433	991	442	197,814	4,978	2,186
6	1,433	989	444	197,370	5,967	2,630
7	1,433	987	446	196,924	6,954	3,076
8	1,433	985	448	196,476	7,939	3,524
9	1,433	982	450	196,025	8,921	3,975
10	1,433	980	453	195,573	9,901	4,427
			(...)			
230	1,433	76	1,356	13,942	143,501	186,058
231	1,433	70	1,363	12,579	143,570	187,421

232	1,433	63	1,370	11,209	143,633	188,791
233	1,433	56	1,377	9,832	143,689	190,168
234	1,433	49	1,384	8,449	143,738	191,551
235	1,433	42	1,391	7,058	143,781	192,942
236	1,433	35	1,398	5,661	143,816	194,339
237	1,433	28	1,405	4,256	143,844	195,744
238	1,433	21	1,412	2,844	143,866	197,156
239	1,433	14	1,419	1,426	143,880	198,574
240	1,433	7	1,426	0	143,887	200,000

8.1.5 Converting a Future Value into an Annuity (Sinking Fund)

With formula (8-2) on page 170 we transformed a given annuity into a future value by multiplying the annuity with the FVAF (future value annuity factor). To do that, we only need the interest rate per period i and the number of periods n.

We can of course reverse this procedure, in order to determine the annuity for a given future value. The way to go is just to divide the future value by the FVAF, the result being the annuity.

The typical application is the sinking fund. A sinking fund is an account being set up to accumulate funds for a specific purpose.

Example 8-10: Sinking fund annuity – quarterly payments

Muck Inc. has decided to set up a sinking fund for the purpose of purchasing some new equipment in 2 years' time. The machine will cost 40,000€. Muck will earn 8 percent interest per year compounded quarterly. What is the annuity to be paid quarterly into the fund?

Step 1: Determine the FVAF from formula (8-2) for 8 percent annually, which is 8%/4 = 2% quarterly.

The periods are now measured in quarters, so that there are 4 x 2 = 8 quarters.

$$FVAF = \frac{(1+i)^n - 1}{i} = \frac{1.02^8 - 1}{0.02} = 8.58296905$$

Step 2: Determine the annuity by dividing the future value of 40,000 by the FVAF:

$$C = 40,000 \div 8.58296902 = 4,660.39€$$

Step 3: Amortization schedule for eight quarters.

For ease of reading, all numbers have been rounded without decimals.

End of period	Deposit Made	Interest earned	Addition to Fund	Accumulated Deposit	Accumulated Interest	Accumulated Fund
	A	$B = F_{n-1} \times i$	$C = A + B$	$D = \sum A$	$E = \sum B$	$F = \sum C$
1	4,660	0	4,660	4,660	0	4,660
2	4,660	93	4,754	9,321	93	9,414
3	4,660	188	4,849	13,981	281	14,263
4	4,660	285	4,946	18,642	567	19,208
5	4,660	384	5,045	23,302	951	24,253
6	4,660	485	5,145	27,962	1,436	29,398
7	4,660	588	5,248	32,623	2,024	34,647
8	4,660	693	5,353	37,283	2,717	40,000

A. At the end of each of the 8 quarters, Muck Inc. saves 4,660€.

B. Interest each year is calculated by multiplying the accumulated fund of the beginning of the period (F_{n-1}) with the interest rate.

C. The quarterly addition to the fund consists of what Muck pays each quarter (A) plus the interest that is earned on the accumulated fund (B).

D. This is the amount that Muck himself has paid into the fund. At the end of the eighth quarter, Muck has saved 37,283€.

E. The total interest earned until period n is shown here. At the end of period 8, Muck has earned total interest of 2,717€.

F. His own saving (D) plus the interest entire earned (E) makes the accumulated fund at the end of each period.

8.2   Understanding the net present value rule

How do we describe and assess an investment?

For the purpose of deciding on the quality of an investment project, we look at the cash flows that an investment decision will produce. An investment is considered a good project if it (analytically) creates value right now (in t=0). It will create value, if *the present value of all anticipated future cash inflows exceed the present value of all anticipated future cash outflows.* The net present value is the present value of the future cash inflows minus the present value of the future cash outflows.

So the Net Present Value rule says:

If the net present value is positive, i.e. NPV > 0, the investment project creates wealth and it can be accepted.

Which variables do we need to determine the NPV?

- First we need to plan the *cash inflows and the cash outflows.* For convenience they should be assumed to occur *at the end of a year.* Going for monthly cash flows would not significantly change the present value of the cash flows. That means for the ease of all calculations, we assume all cash flows to happen at the end of a year.

- In practical applications, we have to determine the **incremental** cash flows which are the consequence of the investment. This means we would have to figure out exactly by how much existing cash flows will **change** just because the investment project is done.

- Then we need a **discount rate**, which is typically the **Cost of Capital**. The Cost of Capital is typically expressed as a **percentage** – it is the minimum rate of return that the project must earn each year. If the project earns more than this minimum rate of return, then the NPV will be positive.

What does the cost of capital represent?

- The discount rate is an investor's desired or minimum rate of return, generally considered to be the investor's opportunity cost of capital.

- In a simplified interpretation, the discount rate is the return of an **alternative investment of the same risk** – the reason why we also call it the **opportunity cost of capital**. In order for the investment project to be good, it has to be **better than the next available alternative**.

- If the investor uses a mix of debt and equity, then we use the **weighted average cost of capital (WACC)**, which is basically the proportional cost of all financing – debt or equity – the company employs.

Example 8-11: Net Present Value 1

Muck Inc. is currently evaluating an investment in a new product costing 10,000€. Anticipated net cash flows are 6,000€ at the end of year 1, and a further 8,000€ at the end of year 2. Muck Inc. has estimated the cost of capital to be 12 percent.

Step 1: Determine the cash flows.

time	t=0	t=1	t=2
cash flow at time t	-10,000	6,000	8,000

Step 2: Discount each cash flow using the discount rate of 12 percent, and add up the present values.

$$-10,000 + \frac{6,000}{1.12} + \frac{7,000}{1.12^2} = 937.5$$

The initial outlay, the capital expenditure of 10,000 (as it is a negative cash flow, it has a negative sign) is already the present value in t=0 – so no need to discount this.

Result: the net present value of the project is positive, so it is a good project.

8.2.1   Interpreting NPV

We use the data from the previous example.

What can we say about the financials of this project? *Mathematically* it is easy to understand the NPV being the present value of all incremental cash flows from the project. But how should we understand NPV *economically*?

Let's try this:

The project earns the 12 percent per period which it has to earn - the minimum required rate of return or Cost of Capital. But that is not all. Actually it earns more than these 12 percent Cost of Capital. The Euro amount it earns **above** the Cost of Capital – the 937.5 – this is the Net Present Value of the project. So the Net Present Value is not a profit in the strict sense, but it is **a financial surplus expressed in monetary terms as a value in t=0**.

To prove these statements, let us just assume the investor does not use equity, but finances the project with loans of 12 percent.

If the investor uses loans at 12 percent interest, he will have to repay any loan and pay any interest with the cash inflows from the project. For this case, let us just figure out **what the maximum amount of loans would be** that the investor can take in t=0 so that he can repay them from the project's future cash flows.

- In t=0 he takes a loan of 6,000/1.12 = 5,357.14€ which he repays (including interest) in t=1 with the 6,000€ he gets in t=1.
- Also in t=0, he takes a second loan of 7,000/1.12² = 5,580.36€, which he repays in full with the 7,000€ cash inflow in t=2.

Let's look at the transactions in a table:

time	t=0	t=1	t=2
Cash flows from the project	− 10,000	6,000	7,000
Loan 1	+5,357.14	−6,000	
Loan 2	+5,580.36	0	− 7,000
Total ∑ from all cash flows	+937.50	0	0

We assumed the investor does not use his own funds, but still the project gives him **an additional cash inflow in t=0 of 937.50€**. This is because the 12 percent loan assumption implies that he gets loans so that he can repay them in full plus interest of 12 percent – and he has still 937.5€ in excess of the financing cost that the project was able to take care of.

8.2.2　Net present value vs. internal rate of return

The internal rate of return is the discount rate r for which the Net Present Value of a cash flow (consisting of an initial cash outlay and future net cash inflows) is exactly zero. We can describe this formally as:

$$NPV = \sum_{t=0}^{n} \frac{cf_t}{(1+r)^t} = 0$$

The internal rate of return is the effective annualized return of a series of cash flows. What does it mean if the project has a Net Present Value of zero?

In **Example** 8-11 the Internal Rate of Return is around 18.9 percent. This can be determined quite easily with Microsoft Excel.

	A	B	C
1	-10,000	+6,000	+7,000
2			
3	=IRR(A1:C1) Result: 18.88% [7]		

The project really earns 18.9 percent – a lot more than the minimum 12 percent which it has to earn as a minimum rate of return. So we can say that a *NPV greater than zero* is **equivalent** as to say that the *Internal Rate of Return is greater than the minimum required rate of return*.

---

[7] For German language Excel, the function would be =IKV(A1:C1)

But beware: we can only use the Internal Rate of Return to assess a single project by comparing it with the minimum rate of return. We cannot use IRR to make exclusive choices between several projects or to rank a number of different projects by their IRR. Even trickier are decision situations for projects that have different lifetimes.[8]

Decision makers shouldn't say "Project A is better than Project B because it has a higher IRR". If they say that, they overlook that Project B might well have a higher NPV, but a lower IRR – as we see in the following example.

Example 8-12: Mutually exclusive projects – NPV and IRR

Muck Inc. is evaluating two mutually exclusive projects, which means only one project can be realised. The table below shows the expected cash flows for the projects.

Project	t=0	t=1	t=2	t=3	t=4
A	-400	164	148	132	116
B	-500	170	206	135	171

Using Excel, we can easily determine the IRR for both projects:

	A	B	C	D	E
1	-400	164	148	132	116
2	-500	170	206	135	171
3	=IRR(A1:E1) Result: 16%		=IRR(A2:E2) Result: 14%		

Comparing the **IRR**, Project A with 16% IRR is a better project than B with an IRR of 14%.

For computing the **NPVs** of the project, we have to know the discount rate (the opportunity cost of capital or minimum rate of return) for the decision maker. Calculating NPVs for different discount rates yield different NPVs:

Minimum return/Cost of Capital	NPV A	NPV B
6%	89,15 €	92,51 €
7%	78,79 €	79,46 €
7.26%	76,18 €	76,18 €
10%	49,81 €	43,02 €

---

[8] Renowned Corporate Finance book will contain and discuss such cases, e.g. Brealey, Myers, Allen: Principles of Corporate Finance; Pike/Neale: Corporate Finance and Investment; Berk/DeMarzo: Corporate Finance.

13%	23,67 €	10,21 €
14%	15,52 €	0,00 €
16%	0,00 €	-19,43 €
18%	-14,55 €	-37,62 €
20%	-28,23 €	-54,69 €

We see that at a discount rate of about 7.26%, both projects are equally favorable. But for discount rates below 7.26%, project B is better because of the higher NPV. For discount rates above 7.26%, Project A has the higher NPV and therefore is considered the better project.

When facing such a situation, the project with a higher NPV should be chosen because there is an inherent reinvestment assumption in the calculation of the IRR. In our calculation, there is an assumption that the cash flows *will be reinvested at the same discount rate* at which they are discounted. In the NPV calculation, the implicit assumption for reinvestment rate is the minimum rate of return or opportunity cost of capital. In IRR, the implicit reinvestment rate assumption is of 16% or 14%. The reinvestment rate of 16% or 14% in IRR is quite unrealistic compared to NPV. This makes the NPV results superior to the IRR results.

The above example illustrated the conflicting results of NPV and IRR due to differing cash flow patterns. The conflicting results can also occur because of the size and investment of the projects. A small project may have low NPV but higher IRR.

A final remark: net present value is an *absolute measure* i.e. it represents the amount of value added or wealth created (or lost) in *monetary terms* by undertaking a project. IRR on the other hand is a *relative measure* i.e. it is the *percentage rate of return* a project offers over its lifespan.

Bibliography

Barker, Richard (2010): On the definitions of income, expenses and profit in IFRS. In: Accounting in Europe 7 (2), S. 147–158.

Devalle, Alain; Magarini, Riccardo (2012): Assessing the value relevance of total comprehensive income under IFRS: an empirical evidence from European stock exchanges. In: International Journal of Accounting, Auditing and Performance Evaluation 8 (1), S. 43–68.

Ding, Y./Jeanjean, T./Stolowy, H. (2008): The impact of firms' internationalization on financial statement presentation: Some French evidence, in: Advances in Accounting, incorporating Advances in International Accounting 24, (2008) 145-156.

Ernst & Young 2015: Accounting for share-based payments under IFRS 2 – the essential guide.

Fiori, Giovanni; Di Donato, Francesca; Macciocchi, Daniele: IFRS and international differences: An empirical analysis on their application worldwide. In: Corporate Ownership and Control 11 (2).

Kieso/Weygandt/Warfield (2014): Financial Accounting IFRS Edition.

Needles B./Powers, M. (2011): International Financial Reporting Standards: An Introduction, 2nd ed.

Nobes, Christopher W.; Stadler, Christian (2015): The qualitative characteristics of financial information, and managers' accounting decisions: evidence from IFRS policy changes. In: Accounting and Business Research 45 (5), S. 572–601.

Penman, Stephen H. (2010): Financial forecasting, risk and valuation: Accounting for the future. In: Abacus 46 (2), S. 211–228.

Pronobis, Paul; Zülch, Henning (2011): The predictive power of comprehensive income and its individual components under IFRS. In: Problems and Perspectives in Management (PPM), Forthcoming.

Roll, Richard (1986): The hubris hypothesis of corporate takeovers. In: Journal of business, S. 197–216.

Seth, Anju; Song, Kean P.; Pettit, Richardson (2000): Synergy, managerialism or hubris? An empirical examination of motives for foreign acquisitions of US firms. In: Journal of international business studies 31 (3), S. 387–405.

Spiceland, Sepe, Nelson: Intermediate Accounting, Vol. 1 & 2.

Weetman, Pauline: Financial accounting. An introduction, latest edition.

Index

17592552R00104

Printed in Poland
by Amazon Fulfillment
Poland Sp. z o.o., Wrocław